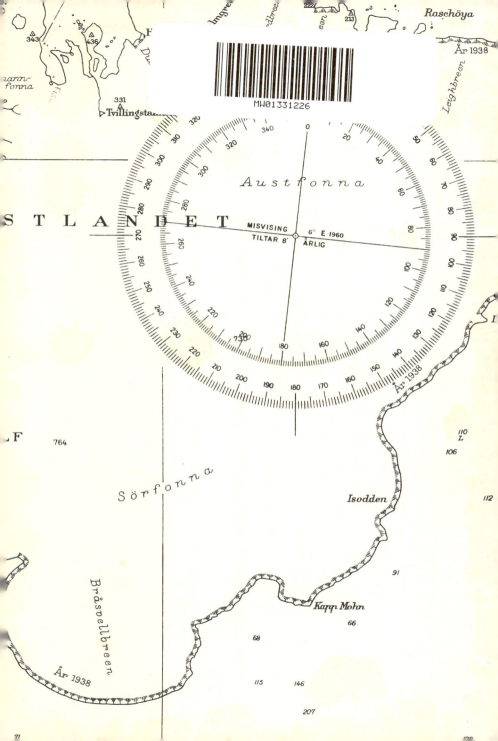

JOURNEY INTO SILENCE

JOURNEY INTO SILENCE

JACK DENTON SCOTT

READER'S DIGEST PRESS
Distributed by
THOMAS Y. CROWELL COMPANY   New York   1976

Copyright © 1976 by Jack Denton Scott

Portions of this book appeared in slightly different form in *Playboy*.

All rights reserved. Except for use in a review, the reproduction or utilization of this work in any form or by any electronic, mechanical, or other means, now known or hereafter invented, including xerography, photocopying, and recording, and in any information storage and retrieval system is forbidden without the written permission of the publisher. Published simultaneously in Canada by Fitzhenry & Whiteside Limited, Toronto.

Designed by Abigail Moseley
Map by George Buctel

Manufactured in the United States of America

Library of Congress Cataloging in Publication Data

Scott, Jack Denton, 1915–
　Journey into silence.
　　1. Svalbard—Description and travel.　2.　Scott, Jack Denton, 1915–　I. Title.
G780.S36　　　919.8'1　　　75-33837
ISBN 0-88349-083-8

1 2 3 4 5 6 7 8 9 10

This is for George Herz
who made this journey possible—
talented poet, gentle man and dear friend.

ACKNOWLEDGMENTS

I am grateful to the following for help in a variety of ways. *Takk* to old friend Per Prag, Director of the Norwegian National Tourist Office in America, whose knowledge of his country is encyclopaedic, his cooperation limitless, his Norwegian character such that a Viking would sit up and take notice. *Takk* also to Geoffrey K. Ward, Director of the Scandinavia Overseas Service, Inc., wishing him good luck with his King's Bay venture; another *takk* to Einar Bergh, Deputy Director, the Norwegian Information Service in the United States, and to William Bauserman, friend and librarian extraordinary, whose sensitivity for the subject helped so much; to my friend and associate Joan Raines who believed, encouraged and forged the way, and a double *takk* to my friend, come hell, high water, ice floes or credit cards, Maria Luisa Scott, who pulled everything together and rowed this ship to shore.

JDS

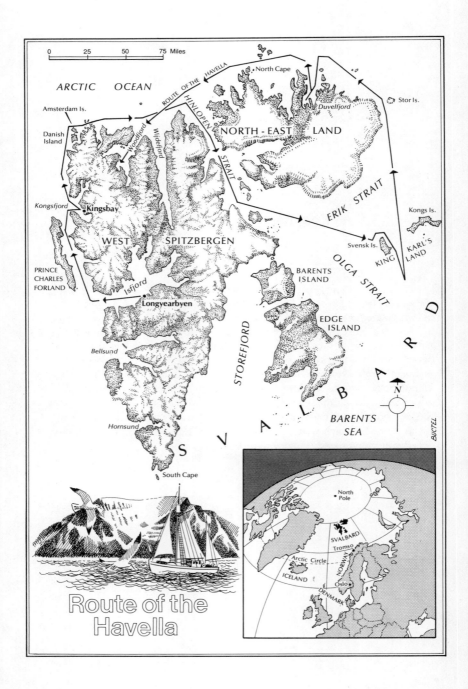

1

It was an offer I couldn't resist.

I would be the first man in more than ten years to see the peaceful, silent land locked behind a towering Chinese Wall Front Glacier.

Chinese Wall Front Glacier.

A monster of solid ice, ten times the height of the twenty-foot-high Great Wall of China, from which it takes its name, it smashes everything in its path in its slow, inexorable glacial stride to the sea. It stands as a gigantic frozen fortress blocking all entry to the land behind it, creating its own Ice Age.

It can also lock land away from the sight of man for decades, keeping secure the secrets and the sanctity of the area.

And I had a chance to travel to just such a glacier, to a lost land on top of the world. The journey began in a deceptively mundane way, with a telephone call from an old friend.

My friend, George Herz, suggested that when I had time I come to his office in New York. "I've got something that will appeal to your weird wanderlust. Way out."

I made it to his office from Connecticut in two hours. Herz sat at his desk unrolling a map. I like to hear a map being unrolled. It creaks and groans as if reluctant to be opened and have its strange places and secrets scanned.

"What've you got?" I asked, knowing that this man never wasted anyone's time, including his own.

"It's a lost arctic lake," he said. "A glacial lake. No one has seen it, or even the area around it for twelve years. You could be the first."

Just the thought of a fresh area that we haven't littered, polluted, and overpopulated is enough to set the imagination afire. The world is so well trampled that no matter where you go—even to the moon—someone has been there before. There are no new lands to conquer, and there is little left unspoiled.

So, suspicious, I asked how it was possible that there could be a lake anywhere on earth that no man had seen for a dozen years.

At that point George Herz first told me about the Chinese Wall Front Glacier that had created the unique situation. He was a man who could tell a lot about the polar world. Then an executive with the Scandinavian Airlines System and a long-time adventurer of the mind, he had been involved in the planning of the first commercial passenger flights across the North Pole.

I knew from earlier conversations what his airline had to do in pioneering the North Pole air lane, and about the seemingly unsolvable navigational problems involving the magnetic North Pole, the polar twilight, and the disappearance of direction at the Pole. In that arctic region ordinary compasses point due south when they should read north, or they go wild. Herz's airline had to find something that would point in one direction and stay there. So their scientists developed the Polar Path Gyro. The size of an orange, it worked like a top; electrically powered, it remained fixed in space for twenty hours. Ordinary maps also were useless, necessitating a change of course every few minutes as the plane flew across one meridian after another.

Progress was further complicated by the fact that all meridians meet at the Pole, where all directions become south. Thus the airline had to develop a new method, the Polar Grid System. This was an accurate chart of the polar regions overprinted with a series of parallel lines. All meridians were ignored except the center line running from Greenwich, England, across the North Pole and on down to the South Pacific. The direction of the line was north, grid north, remaining north even after the plane had passed the geographic North Pole and was technically going south. The chart was the key to that amazing flight across the top of the world, inaugurated on February 24, 1957, with a plane flying from Los Angeles to Copenhagen.

People on the ground had to help. There were flight watches from five special radio stations widely spaced in the Arctic, each with a ground-wave transmitter with a range of seven hundred miles, the first time ground-wave stations were used on such a large scale. They were furnished with the plane's position checks, and the pilot then used them as a navigational cross-check. They also fed the pilot weather and other ground data.

Herz's airline did in sixteen hours what explorers Fridtjof Nansen, Robert E. Peary, and Roald Amundsen had taken a year to accomplish. And those explorers had traversed just a small part of the Arctic. The airline regularly hopped from Tokyo to Copenhagen.

I thought of all this as I listened to my friend describing that arctic lake lost from human sight. I also thought of Peary's dogs taking thirty-six brutal days to drag sleds from Ellesmere Island, west of Greenland, to the North Pole.

Not least, I thought about myself, as I stood listening,

wondering if I really knew very much about what made me tick, what made me want to go to the far places. I knew this much: I considered the seeking more important than the finding, which was at least a small step ahead in looking into my own mind and motivations.

I remembered, too, the thoughts of James Whittaker, the first American to reach the top of Mt. Everest. He said that he liked the peace of the high places. In the stillness there he remembered how his pack frame creaked, the snow complaining beneath his feet. No one talked much, he said. They were working too hard. Sometimes an icefall broke away from a rock cliff and rumbled and roared down the pitch. Then he knew he was in his element and part of it was the realization that danger lurked everywhere, that he was putting his life on the line.

He went to Mt. Everest because of the challenge, because he wanted to see if he could reach the top. Afterward he said you don't really conquer such a mountain. What you conquer is yourself.

Maybe that was what I had been trying to do. I didn't do it in the jungles of India, when I lived with the natives, or in the Philippine rain forests, or in the other off-the-beaten-path areas to which I had gone. But I did believe with Whittaker that man is better off when he meets the challenge offered by the wild places. "Man needs challenges," the mountain climber said. "That's the nature of him."

Or perhaps he needs to clear his perspective by getting out of the cage of civilization, to look back at himself and what he has been. One thing I knew for certain right now: Because of his involvement with the polar flights and his own interest in the north and its people, George Herz would be sure of his facts.

A slender, controlled man with a good brain and brown eyes that snapped with enthusiasm, he had that convincing personality that just a few gifted salesmen have. Only he wasn't selling me anything. He was just giving facts to a friend he knew was interested in the offbeat places and circumstances of the world. This was both, unusual place *and* circumstance.

Herz said that a friend of his, a Norwegian pilot, had been told by seal hunters and codfishermen, who traveled in those lonely reaches, that several warm summers and mild winters had melted parts of that land-locking glacier. The vast cliffs of ice had reached the sea, which undercut them, and large pieces were breaking off, calving into the sea. At the rate that this was happening, it was almost certain that a channel would be opened through which a small ship could pass. Herz couldn't go himself, but he had the name of a shipowner in Tromsø, a Norwegian city above the Arctic Circle, who could arrange transportation. If I was interested in chartering the boat.

Interested! Visiting an area unmarked by man was an opportunity that no one concerned with the survival of his senses could pass up. But where was this place? Was it a Mt. Everest situation? Or could an ordinary man like myself get to it without mounting an expedition?

We looked at the Arctic Ocean and the Barents Sea trembling beneath us, wild even on a map. Exotic names leaped up at me, Lofoten, Hammerfest, Vardø, Kjelvik. Then each of us laid a hand flat on the map to keep it from snapping back into a roll. Spread out, the map's continents, countries, mountains, lakes, rivers, and oceans looked like a palette upon which an artist had dreamily dabbed colors.

Maps are for dreamers. I have a world map under glass on a three-by-five-foot coffee table in my living room that offers me more entertainment than any book or television. In fact, I do not have a television set, believing that it puts restraints and blinders on restive men who dream.

Now as we stood holding the map down in his New York office, Herz, another dreamer, ran his right forefinger like a surfaced whale across the vast open space of the Barents Sea, stopping at a bleak point on the upper corner. There his finger teetered as if it was balancing on top of the world. Which it was.

His finger rested on oblong blue markings, islands forlornly floating far, far north of Norway in a vast circle of water consisting of the Greenland Sea, the Barents Sea, and the Arctic Ocean.

He grinned as he saw my expression. "Join the club. No region, the sources of the Nile, deepest Africa, the high Himalayas, or even the moon, has excited so many explorers."

He took his finger off the map. "I'll tell you about this place in a minute." He stood looking at the islands lost in the sea.

"A relentless place," he said suddenly, "that frozen ocean that surrounds the North Pole. But it has captured the curiosity and imagination of man for twenty-three centuries, ever since the Greek Pytheas of Massilia sailed from Britain to Iceland in 335 B.C. He reported that he saw a great ocean frozen solid and was called a liar."

I could feel an old sickness returning, almost a dizziness, like standing on a sheer cliff looking down, emotion bringing slight nausea and excitement. The adventurers of the far north were my earliest heroes. I had been to Norway, sailed along its coast. In a boring world full of enslaved spirits, I had yearned to go out far beyond Norway and its tourist circuit and retrace the steps of some of the great ones—Byrd, Peary, Nansen, Amundsen. But so far it had mostly been the same kind of finger exercise on a map that we were now doing.

I was using restraint. I wanted to hear about the place. Herz knew me pretty well and looked at me soberly. "Yeah," he said quietly. "Life is more than television." And he told me about Svalbard.

Old Icelandic annals state that Svalbard was first discovered by Norsemen in 1194. In the ancient Norse book *Landnámabok*, it was recorded that from Langanes on the northeastern coast of Iceland it is "four days sailing to Svalbard [land of the cold coasts] at the northernmost limits of the ocean."

Four centuries later, lured by tales of vast riches, two ships under the command of Willem Barents sailed from Holland looking for a shorter route to China. Rather than sail around Africa, Barents decided to short-cut along the north coast of Asia. On June 9, 1596, the Dutchman sighted an island and anchored off it. Some of his sailors killed a polar bear, and Barents named the island Bear Island, which remains its name. On June 17 they saw more land with towering snow-capped mountain peaks. They called it Spitsbergen, "the land of the pointed peaks."

Today the twenty-odd islands in that arctic archipelago are known by both names, Svalbard and Spitsbergen, although the largest island is actually Spitsbergen. All of the islands lie in the Arctic Ocean between 74° and 81° N latitude and between 10° and 35° longitude, 10 degrees and about 400 nautical miles from the North Pole. Their total land area is 23,958 square miles, one-fifth the size of the mother country, Norway.

The islands were the jumping-off place for many explorers hoping to reach the Pole by various means. Some made it. Some did not. Salomon August Andrée, a Swedish scientist, tried it in 1897 in a balloon. He died on one of the islands. American Walter Wellman attempted it in 1909, using a flimsy aircraft, which he wrecked in Svalbard. He was rescued by a party of Norwegians from Tromsø.

The archipelago lies squarely in the northwesterly part of the large continental platform between the polar basin and the continent to the south. Most of the islands have glaciers and mountains; one mountain, Newton Toppen, peaks at 5,630 feet.

"And no natives," George Herz said. "Maybe a thousand Norwegians and twice that many Russians working the coal mines. The island you'll be looking for is the second largest,

Nordaustlandet. That's about all I know. But you'll be an expert by the time you get back from this one."

Good man. He didn't say "if" you get back. Not George, the positive thinker.

Even for the foolhardy, the daring, and the driven, adventure requires a focal point. Dictionaries define adventure as an undertaking of a hazardous nature, or an unusual experience or course of events marked by excitement and suspense. To get involved with an adventure such as this one required more than the usual focal point. I needed an alibi to prove to others and to myself why a grown man would undertake this adventure—would seemingly act so irresponsibly immature. Focal points and alibis sometimes merge. Find the Northwest Passage. The North Pole. The South Pole. Be the first to go by foot. By boat. By dog sled. By pony. By balloon. By plane. Float the Pacific on a raft to prove men had done it before.

To my way of thinking, I had, at least at this time in our century, a most valid reason pulling me. Find a lost arctic lake, not seen in twelve years. But more than that. At this point man has overproduced not only his own kind, but everything else, bringing his noise and destruction everywhere. What would I be getting away from? Cities, forcing me to inhale poison gas, to walk filthy streets, to travel dangerous, dirty subways, to see garbage on the streets, to face noise so loud and constant that one's hearing is impaired and nerves are jangled, to worry about having one's house burglarized, or the fear of mugging—

Or was I overconvincing myself to get out where isolation was an insulator? I wondered what had happened to that lake in more than a decade of being locked away from the world? What about the area around this icebound Shangri-La? What about the animals there? How do wild animals react when they have never seen a human being? Would there be birds? Flowers? What did the glacier leave behind? Would the lake have fish? Salmon?

What would the texture of that silence be like? How would it affect me? The men with me? Was there really such a thing as pure silence?

Would someone get there before I could? Herz doubted it. Only seal hunters and codfishermen would know about it and they did not have my kind of curiosity pushing them. They were hardworking men who looked at the north country in terms of their livelihood, not as a place for the fun and games of being somewhere first. They were men used to silence. They would not go looking for a new silence.

Preparation would not be too involved. The best months were those in which I would go, July, August, and September. There would be constant sun, Midnight Sun. The temperature would probably not drop below thirty-five degrees. But it could be cold on the deck of a ship on the north seas. Abercrombie and Fitch in New York told me about the Grenfell coat designed for an Everest expedition. Virtually waterproof, lined with thick wool pile, with an inner liner of plastic, double zipper, buttons, belt, and a lined hood. Yet it wasn't heavy. There were black ten-inch Top Sider boots that would slip over shoes and had suction soles to keep you standing on a tilting or slippery deck. A wool cap with pile earflaps that could be tied up on top when not needed. Sheepskin gloves. Raingear. Good sunglasses to protect the eyes from ice and sea glare. Heavy walking shoes with corrugated soles to prevent slipping when ashore. Buy a sweater in Norway. Best in the world. Other items were required, but there wouldn't be too much gear to lug along.

Finances? Ah, there we get complicated. I will not list the boring details, except to mention that the credit card could well be this century's magic carpet. The day of reckoning arrives of course, but you try not to think about those moments that take the fun out of life. They can always be mastered. The debit column is balanced by the profit of an unusual experience.

Memories can be more precious than money in the bank. The sad thing is not to have any.

When doubts assail, I shore up my spirits by remembering Supreme Court Justice William O. Douglas saying, "The richness of life is found in adventure. It develops self-reliance and independence—then life teems with excitement."

Passport? Norway does not require a visa from Americans.

Transportation to this last frontier? On the surface it looked simple. But simple is a slippery word.

I would first fly by jet to Copenhagen, Denmark; continue by prop plane to a point in northern Norway; then take a bus through farm country to Tromsø, capital of the bleak country above the Arctic Circle. I would then board a coastal steamer and sail to Longyearbyen, the tiny coal-mining community. There a specially constructed fifty-seven-foot diesel ketch would be waiting. It would take me across the ice-cluttered sea, skirted by uninhabited glacial islands, to the lost lake of Svalbard.

2

Reality caught up with me shortly after I left Copenhagen in the two-motored plane. I knew I was on my way to remote country when those two engines roared, the plane making wind-whipping sounds as if it was coming apart. And then the hard take-off, the pulse-racing time needed to get up, then level off, and the harder wheel-bouncing landing at an airport that looked like a mistake. The runway tarmac was cracked and too short, and feathered grass, growing out of the cracks, waved in the wash of the props as we came in.

I had completed the second step of my northward journey. This was Norway's Bardufoss, farming country, with a military base nearby, about halfway between the towns of Narvik and Tromsø.

Here, at Bardufoss bus station I saw my first Lapps, a man and his wife, drinking coffee and talking animatedly in a language that sounded oriental. They were short and heavy with broad faces; only the light complexion, the ruddy color, the apple cheeks made me realize that they weren't Mongolian. Or were they? No one seems to know. Seeing them put me squarely in time and place. The woman had on a traditional costume, an apron over a billowy skirt and a lace cap, the man was dressed in a loose blue and red jacket and a cap with a red tassel.

The Lapps are a nomadic people, though some of them have become fishermen and farmers. They are found only in the northern sectors of Norway, Sweden, Finland, and Russia. A race apart, they are noted for their domesticated herds of reindeer, using the animal for about everything—transportation, food, clothing, even its hide for their dwellings. They are tough, resilient people, following the reindeer on their migrations, living in tents and crude huts. Except for their coloring they reminded me of the Eskimos. But there was something more dramatic about them.

There wouldn't even be rugged Lapps where I was going, just a few people in what passed for civilization in Svalbard, the mountain coal mines on the very edge of the wilderness I would enter.

It was incongruous that a prosaic bus would take me on this third leg to Tromsø, to catch a coastal steamer that would go as far north as it could—as incongruous as taking a subway to begin a rocket trip to the moon.

And this was a prosaic bus. Faded yellow, mud-streaked, I couldn't even tell what make or model it was, but all of us riding in it instantly knew that it was old. It rattled and it squealed when it lurched around curves. The middle-aged driver had blue eyes hard as pebbles that skeptically watched the road. He sat stolidly at the wheel, answering in monosyllables, without turning his head, the few questions that were asked by the passengers. Calm, sure of himself, taciturn, he seemed symbolic of his nationality.

Despite the bus and the road, he made me feel that we would make it. For about ten miles the road was blacktopped; but beyond that it was unpaved. The winter had heaved and pitted it, and I literally began to get the feel of the country we were traveling through. It had only a tenuous grasp on civilization. The land looked thin, rocky; the hard-won crops seemed to consist mainly of hay, potatoes, and a few carrot patches. I later learned that only 2.7 percent of the land is tillable. In Norway most of the food comes from the sea. Norwegians are such superb fishermen that their country, despite its population of only 3.5 million spread out over 119,240 square miles, ranks third in the world in the production of fish and has the fourth largest merchant marine fleet.

They live farther north than anyone else; the southern tip of their country is the same latitude as northern Labrador, its northern edge on a line with the northern coast of Alaska. Two-thirds of the way up the coast the Arctic Circle cuts across the long, narrow land, bordered by the Atlantic for more than a thousand miles. Seventy percent of the country seems to be rock, and most of that harsh terrain is uninhabited, the Norwegians living only near fjords, the shores of lakes, in valleys, and along the coast—"Betwixt the hills and the mountains and out by the sea," as one of their poets wrote.

It is not the bitter land it appears to be. Warmed by southwesterly winds, its climate is also kept livable by the mild ocean current of the Gulf Stream, which surges up from the Gulf of Mexico. Over 100,000 islands and great rock formations protect much of the coast from the brunt of Atlantic winds and storms.

Although the sea and the mountains have forged a hardy people accustomed to strenuous outdoor labor and activities, Norwegians are also able to enjoy the luxury of the cheapest electrical power in the world. Swift mountain rivers supply inexhaustible hydroelectric power, 30 billion kilowatt-hours a year for the small population.

The rest of the passengers on the bus were probably fishermen and farmers and their wives, some wearing sweaters and shawls, others in their Sunday best. One brawny woman, her fair hair almost white, carried three fat brown hens in a crate. The chickens clucked constantly, a pleasant, lulling sound as we jogged along. The passengers did not talk to one another, but sat staring out of the windows as if they had never made the trip before.

Farm families were in the fields, men and boys with their shirts off, women and girls stripped to their bras, all haying, pitchforking it into piles and the backs of horse-drawn wagons. In several fields women were passing a coffeepot. It was a happy sight. Togetherness is a cup of coffee in a sunlit hayfield. Every small farm had a horse, some three or four cows. The farmhouses all had thick sod roofs that seemed to have grown there, several had trees sprouting from that sod. For some reason I do not understand, it all gave me a sudden sharp pain of nostalgia. For a simple world I would never know?

We rumbled to a stop at Vollan, at the head of Balsfjord, and the white-blonde with her clucking chickens, and about half the other passengers got off. North, the road forked to Alta, west to Tromsø.

It took nearly five hours to make the trip from Bardufoss to the end of the third leg, Tromsø, capital of the Norwegian Arctic. Bit by bit, the harness that held me to what I had left behind was dropping off.

The city's boat-filled harbor and stern gray houses swam into view on its island, Tromøya, for which it was named. We entered across steel hanging like a great strand of a spider web, the largest suspension bridge in northern Europe, 1,036 meters, linking Tromøya to the mainland. The city, with its 864 square miles, is the largest in area in Norway, and, as signs of occupation going back 4,500 years attest, has been inhabited longer than any other Norwegian city.

From my vantage point high on the bridge, the town didn't

look that permanent against the implacable backdrop of the sea. Some cities sit cozily by the ocean, peaceful as the scene on a tourist postcard. But the cold menace of the sea was the striking note here. From this distance Tromsø seemed about to be engulfed by its harbor. Gulls hung above it without flapping a wing. It was a seascape brought alive by the ships moving in, grunting like great beasts in pain. For me that noise would be the sound of the city.

Beyond were mountains lightly mantled with snow. As we got closer I could see large buildings, probably hotels, as well as churches and municipal structures. The colors of some houses, red and yellow, flashed up at me. The view was pulled into focus as we drew closer, the loose settlement sitting by the sea became a city with museums, restaurants, resthouses, and a shopping center.

I remembered that the German battleship *Tirpitz* was defiantly sunk in Tromsø Harbor in World War II, and that here on June 7, 1940, King Hakon and his government left on the cruiser *Devonshire* to carry on the fight against the Germans from England. That fight resulted in half the Norwegian merchant marine fleet being sunk, with the loss of four thousand seamen.

Most important to me was the fact that Tromsø is the gateway to the extreme north, the last place where people gather, the jumping-off point. I shouldn't have been surprised to find that about thirty thousand people lived here, a little over two hundred miles above the Arctic Circle. Although it had the feel of a frontier settlement, old and new blended well, houses being mainly unpainted frame structures silvered by weather. Most displayed flowerpots on windowsills, geraniums and stocks. Everywhere you looked was water, cold, domineering, gray even with the sun on it.

Strangely, it was the flowers that made me spend a couple of bad hours looking inwardly. Suddenly I felt as alien as those summer flowers in this settlement teetering on the edge of the iced-in north. I was sure that when I got to know them, when the veneer of the stranger wore off, that Norwegians would be friendly people. But my impression now was that they were like their land, cold, distant. No one on the streets nodded or spoke to me. There weren't any tourist ships in town and so I obviously was a conspicuous outlander in a place where every citizen not only knew every other, but each was part of a proud population that stood as a buffer against the bleak no-man's-land to the north. Perhaps there was resentment that I wasn't part of that buffer.

My lonely stranger status would change abruptly, for in a day or two ships would arrive with other strangers who would board the steamship *Lyngen*. But as I walked the streets alone and watched the traffic in Tromsø Harbor I was uneasy, feeling that perhaps too soon I would be aboard a small craft in the wildest ocean on earth with a few men who might not even talk to me.

When you travel the far places you often do this. Jump the gun on what may lie ahead. It's a mistake. You also often look back at what you have just left and wonder about the mentality involved in walking away from comforts and security to move among strangers, seeking answers to questions that may have no answers.

I thought of the ice in the north seas that must be dangerous even in these summer months, and, as it sometimes does, the thought built a bridge to other summer ice that brought danger.

Freak ice. In India's jungle heat. I was in the central province, Madhya Pradesh, my focal point that time to study the tiger in its habitat. My father had been a naturalist and I was born with the infection.

It was dark, a cloudy day, and we were gathered in a *dak* bungalow trying to decide whether I should go out and sit in a tree in a certain tiger's territory and watch for him. My guide, *shikari* Rao Naidu, thought we were going to have a storm. A pompous Indian, a forest contractor there to buy trees, who was supposed to know the region, said decisively, "Not possible! Those clouds will go."

So, against his better judgment, my *shikari* agreed to take me to the tree.

I sat high in its branches with an Indian, a toothless, nut-brown old man, an aboriginal, dressed only in soiled turban and loincloth. Although this was its territory, the tiger didn't come. But the rain did.

Suddenly it let loose from the sky in great, blinding sheets. Thunder grumbled. The rain stopped as if by someone snapping a switch. Then, gently at first, it began to hail. Hail. In India? "Not possible!" I wished that forest contractor weather expert was there in the tree with me. I looked at the old Indian. His face was squeezed in a grimace. He was frightened. He had every right to be.

The hail grew in size. In seconds it was the size of golf balls. It fell steadily. I held the thick foam pad that we had been sitting on over our heads.

As suddenly as it began the hail stopped.

I had sore knees and legs for days from that ice from the sky. The shoeless old Indian's feet were pretty badly cut.

Except for that experience I knew nothing about wild ice. But I had the feeling that I had some knowledge coming up.

I checked into the Grand Hotel with no help from two overage bellboys who lounged at the entrance. The place smelled sourly of cabbage, my room was too small, but there was an air of excitement, of history, about the old hotel that made up for some of its shortcomings. I doubt though that its romantic air could have sustained me for a week.

The shipowner, whose diesel ketch was going to be waiting for me in Svalbard, sent his representative to the hotel to answer questions and fill me in on sailing schedules. Wilhelm Bolin was thin, young, with sparse blond hair and startled blue eyes. He had a soft, pleasant personality and a patient way that made me immediately like him. He clutched an old-fashioned double-strapped black briefcase as if it contained rare documents. In a way it did; it held the answers to about any question I asked.

After dinner of overcooked mutton and greasy undercooked potatoes, Bolin smiled weakly and said, "The Grand isn't noted for its food. But we have a good cook on the *Havella*, our ketch, which you'll board in Spitsbergen."

We talked briefly about my schedule. I would sail on the *Lyngen* at midnight three days hence. Dependent upon weather, it would take about four days to get to Longyearbyen in Svalbard, which half the time Bolin called Spitsbergen. I liked the sound of the Norwegian "Svalbard" better than the Dutch "Spitsbergen" and stayed with it, which seemed to unsettle Bolin until he followed my lead. But he didn't talk much about Svalbard, telling me that the crew on the ketch were the experts and would fill me in. But he did talk about Tromsø, the seasons that ruled life in the town, and about the explorers who had left from here.

"We live off the sea," he said. "Shipping, shipyards, fisheries. In our harbor express coastal steamers, local ferries, and some few tourist liners that make this their last port of call mix with fishing vessels from all over the north."

He talked for a while of what made the town tick—fish, seal oil factories, and tanneries—said that it was famous for its boots and used to make the best whaling vessels before most of the whales were killed off.

"You wouldn't believe it," he said somberly, "but we are warmer here than they are in Oslo. In winter rarely does it dip to fifteen below and in summer it is not unusual for us to have seventy-seven degrees."

The days are long, he said, meaning it literally as I was to discover immediately. When you get above the Arctic Circle it is daylight around the clock from May through August. But that constant summer sun is off-balanced by no light at all from November 25 to January 21, except from the weird Northern Lights that occasionally flash across the sky.

"*Døgnavild* is what we call the time right now when we can't tell day from night," Bolin said. "When we have the polar blackness we call it *mørketiden*, the murky time."

He talked of the murky time somewhat fearfully, telling me that during those two months when the sun does not rise above the horizon, except for an hour of grayish twilight at noon, some people come apart. They become sour, edgy, argumentative, the community slows down, people are always tired, their work capacity is reduced.

Bolin spoke of the dark time grudgingly, as if he was exposing a weakness of his people that it was no business of mine to know anything about. I remained silent all through his discourse on the darkness. He spoke of Kaare Rodahl, a noted physiologist and northern researcher, who said that the polar night had the tendency to bring out the least desirable elements in human behavior—jealousy, envy, egotism, suspicion, irritability.

"It's maybe the lack of sleep," Bolin said, eying me speculatively, probably wondering why I wasn't hurling questions at him about this strange time. "During the murky months when you wake up you don't know if it is time to go to work or go back to sleep. Nature's clock is all mixed up. You have to live by the artificial one on your wrist."

He said that some people were even more dependent upon the artificial, that the sales of tranquilizers, sleeping pills, even pep pills rise during the two dark months, as do accidents and illness, most of it psychosomatic. Some people even lose a sense of proportion. One winter a man took off in his snowmobile in his shirt sleeves and froze to death.

Mørketiden is also fought with light, the abundant, cheap

electricity, people turning lights on everywhere at all times, in gardens, on gates, doorways, windows. Some fight the dark with activity, driving a hundred miles to a restaurant that is open all night; others save their vacation time for those two sunless months and leave Norway.

Oslo psychiatrist Karl Hartviksen believes that the murky time may have made Norwegians above the Arctic Circle more forgiving and tolerant than other people. In the real north people realize that they cannot rule nature, so they don't expect man to rule his own nature, which is even more formidable.

Bolin remarked that psychiatrists have an answer for everything. The real answer he said was *Soldag*. "Sun Day," he said. "We wait for that day. When the sun rises over the horizon again we close schools and offices, have sun feasts."

He looked at me, severely, I thought. "You may end up with an even stranger affliction than we have during the dark days. You may get sick of the sun."

I didn't get sick of it, at least right away, for this was all too new, but I did have trouble sleeping in Tromsø, especially when I found it a town where no one seemed to sleep during the normal time. Once, close to two A.M., a band was playing in the sunlit streets, people were strolling, workmen were repairing a water main, boats hooted in the harbor like hounds on a trail, gulls were in a constant spiral above the town. I wondered about the birds. Did they handle this permanent sunlight more gracefully than men?

When I did manage to get to sleep, I awoke at ten A.M., was out on the streets at eleven. The whole place looked deserted. If Tromsonians stayed up all night and rested during the day, as it seemed, when did anyone get anything done? This was a strange, turned-around world. I'd do more thinking about that Midnight Sun on the diesel ketch in the Arctic Ocean, when I had more time to concentrate on a single subject.

Right now I wandered Tromsø, trying to get the feel of this last town that I would see. It also was the opportunity to get that Norwegian sweater. Everywhere you go you see women knitting, in restaurants, hotel lobbies, waiting in cars. It is a matter of national pride that the real Norwegian sweater is not made in a factory. It must be made by hand in vivid patterns and shades that change in each district of the country. It is said that the sweaters are warmer than a down jacket and will last a lifetime. Fortunately, the sweaters are sold in shops.

One shopkeeper seemed insulted when I innocently asked if the pile of gaudy sweaters I was looking at were handmade.

He raised his eyes, shocked. "How else?" he said and strode stiffly away to attend to another customer who didn't need attention. Sweater shopping, I made the rounds of all of the shops. It was obvious that tourists did come this far north. On display were sealskin boots, jackets, gloves, and a cunning array of trinkets made from sealskin and whalebone, hand-knit caps, mittens, stockings, superb glass and ceramics.

One shop had a polar bear skin with a hi-fi unit in its head. I had seen polar bears in zoos, always stretched out on rocks overlooking a pool, or agitatedly pacing in their cages, but I had never really realized what huge animals they were. This one must have been eight feet long and weighed over five hundred pounds. The rug occupied one entire section of the shop. I was in the white bear's country now and would soon see one full-mounted, rearing before another shop, and skins tanned in different fashions, with full heads, mouths open, flat, without heads. But whoever had worked on this skin had imagination.

Seeing me staring at the polar bear skin, the owner of the shop came over and clicked on the hi-fi unit in the head. Strains of the "Blue Danube" came lilting out. The shopkeeper's eyes were so blue that they were unreal, the irises floating like flower petals. He talked at length in his pleasant Norwegian-English of the local taxidermist, who he claimed was Norway's best, and urged me to go to his shop and look at his collection. He spoke enthusiastically of the polar bear champ, Henry Rudi, who had killed seven hundred bears. I must have looked startled, for he immediately went into detail about the hard life of the trappers in the far arctic, living alone in huts for years, and reminded me that the record of seven hundred bears was for a lifetime. Henry Rudi had spent over twenty years in Spitsbergen. "He saw his own brother killed by a wounded walrus," the shopkeeper said.

Once, he said, Rudi had returned to Tromsø from several years in Spitsbergen with over one hundred polar bear skins. He took over an entire hotel and gave free rooms and meals to everybody. Two weeks later the skins were sold, the money gone, and Henry Rudi went back to his cabin in Spitsbergen.

Spitsbergen, said the shopkeeper, was the end of the world.

3

The spare man in stone standing ten-feet-tall in Tromsø's main square had on a parkalike garment and no hat. His hair looked as if it could have been grizzled and lay almost flat against his bony head. This, with a prominent, flaring nose and lean features, gave him a hawkish look, which wasn't misleading. Roald Amundsen was aloof, alone, one of the rare ones. A dreamer who did things.

Bolin had talked about him all through dinner. Amundsen was Norway's folk hero, the giant who had accomplished what man had dreamed of for over four centuries, finding the Northwest Passage. One of the last who attempted it before Amundsen set out was John Franklin, who vanished with 134 men. Sixty other expeditions had also failed.

Roald Amundsen's family wanted him to study medicine, but he had gotten his first taste of the Arctic and the sea at twenty-one, when he signed on the *Magdalena* as an ordinary seaman. That voyage had convinced him of his future. When his mother, who had constantly goaded him to become a doctor, died in 1893, Amundsen virtually left the land behind him.

He prepared himself for the sea by studying navigation at the merchant marine school in Antwerp, and, to get his sea legs, even signed on the seal-hunting vessel *Jason*, and spent nine rough, bloody months in the Arctic Ocean. His next step in gaining solid experience was to try to join Baron de Gerlache's *Belgica* on its expedition to the Antarctic. He was accepted as a mate. *Belgica* never made it to its destination, because it could not penetrate the vast fields of pack ice, but the ship received the dubious honor of being the first ever to spend an entire winter frozen in Antarctic ice. The crew of the *Belgica* finally freed her by actually sawing the ship out.

Approaching his goal methodically, for he had always had much more than mere Arctic expeditions in mind, Amundsen got ready for his next adventure by taking courses in physics and earth magnetism at universities in Norway and Germany.

Then, in Tromsø, he found the *Gjøa*, a forty-seven-ton herring sloop that met his exacting specifications. Borrowing the money to buy the sloop and put her in good sailing shape, Amundsen took her north to try her out in the ice, then brought the *Gjøa* back to Tromsø for further repairs and new fittings. He ran out of money, but managed to convince three businessmen of Fredrikstad that his expedition was commercially worthwhile. They financed his search for the Northwest Passage.

He sailed in the *Gjøa* on June 17, 1903, stopping to take on additional supplies near Thule, Greenland, and then went into the straits of the Canadian archipelago. Amundsen had selected his vessel wisely. It did not draw much water and could get through channels so narrow and shallow that there were mere inches to spare.

On September 12, they reached King William Land, not far from the magnetic North Pole, in the center of the ice where the

Franklin expedition had disappeared. Amundsen decided just to winter here. But the ice held him for two years.

The *Gjøa* finally broke free of that ice in August 1905, but was again clutched by it near Herschel Island, where Amundsen had to spend the third winter. But by the end of August 1906, he had brought the *Gjøa* into the harbor of Nome, Alaska, on the Bering Strait. It was the first ship to sail the entire length of the Northwest Passage, the northern sea route from the Atlantic to the Pacific.

From that point on Amundsen became the durable hero of his country. He then headed for the North Pole, but made an abrupt switch and started south when he heard that Robert Peary had reached the Pole on April 6, 1909. Two years later, Amundsen and four of his men planted Norway's flag at the South Pole.

By July 18, 1918, Amundsen had another expedition under way. In the *Maud* he sailed to Cape Chelyuskin in Siberia, fixing its position as the most northerly point in Asia. The *Maud* was locked in ice for two winters north of Siberia, but in the fall of 1920 Amundsen brought her into the harbor at Nome. He thus became the first to sail both the Northeast and Northwest passages, to pass both the Eurasian and American continents.

Amundsen then, with the American Lincoln Ellsworth financing and accompanying him, pioneered in exploring the north by air, taking two twin-engine seaplanes as far as 88° North. One plane crashed, the other barely made it back after being grounded under treacherous conditions for twenty-one days.

Undaunted, Amundsen then made the world's first transpolar flight in the dirigible *Norge*, flying from Spitsbergen to Teller, Alaska.

Roald Amundsen made his last flight two years later, attempting to rescue Umberto Nobile. Nobile took off for the

Pole in the spring of 1928 in the airship *Italia*, but he was inexperienced and crashed. So did Amundsen, somewhere off Spitsbergen. His body was never found.

Norwegians can still recite the memorial address Fridtjof Nansen gave for Amundsen:

"And then, when his life's work was accomplished, he returned to the Arctic . . . and found an unknown grave under the clean sky of the ice world.

"But from that great white silence, his name will shine out in the glow of the Northern Lights to inspire the youth of our country.

"It is men with courage, determination, and strength like his that give us confidence in the future. The world is still young that rears such sons. . . ."

It was fitting that Fridtjof Nansen should have made that address. An even more famous Norwegian than Amundsen, it was Nansen who had inspired Amundsen in his youth, actually made him what he was.

It all began in 1884, when Eskimos found the wreckage of a ship on the southwest coast of Greenland. It was identified as part of the *Jeannette*, which had been lost north of Siberia.

An American, George W. De Long, a lieutenant in the United States Navy, had a theory that the polar continent was not exactly at the North Pole, but on one side of it. Believing that a ship sailing through open water along the Arctic shore could reach the Pole without trouble, he mounted an expedition in 1879 in the *Jeannette*. A wooden sailing vessel with auxiliary steam, she was not designed for polar ice fields. Although she was well braced inside and had her hull armored with thick planking, she was helpless in the grip of the mighty ice pack. And De Long was wrong. There was no open sea; the shore was not ice-free and could not be navigated. The *Jeannette* drifted in the ice for over a year before it chewed her to death. Of the expedition's thirty men, ten survived. De Long himself died of starvation on an Arctic island.

Henrik Mohn, the widely respected head of the Norwegian Meteorological Institute, thought that this wreckage of the *Jeannette* recovered in Greenland had drifted with the ice from Siberia across the Arctic sea and into the current along the coast of Greenland and its southern tip. Unlike De Long, Mohn did not believe that the circumpolar area had a great land mass, and thought that what it actually contained was just a frozen sea into which flowed various currents.

New, imaginative thinking, it was immediately discounted by experts worldwide. It was widely believed, by those pseudo Arctic explorers who had peeked at the polar basin from a safe distance, that there was a polar continent.

Fridtjof Nansen, the man who was to become Amundsen's idol and spur him into action, whose name Norway and the world would remember, was then a young biologist at the Bergen Museum in Oslo. He was certain Mohn was right and began planning his life around that belief.

Nansen had become interested in the far north shortly after graduating from Oslo University with a degree in zoology. On his twenty-first birthday he made a trip to the Greenland Sea in the sealer, *Viking*. He saw the vast Greenland Ice Cap from a distance. It fired his imagination and even at that age he began to plan.

Nothing much had come of exploring all the other ideas and polar routes, Nansen reasoned. It was only sensible to investigate Mohn's theory. No one else had developed anything nearly as worthy of thought and action.

"If an ice floe could drift right across the unknown region," Nansen speculated, "that drift might be enlisted in the service of exploration—" His plan was laid.

The few who claimed to know the Arctic, such as British

Admiral Sir Leopold McClintock and American General Adolphus Greely, called Nansen not only wrong but foolhardy and reckless.

General Greely was especially contemptuous of Nansen. He had led an unsuccessful expedition to the Arctic ten years before and considered himself knowledgeable. "Probably some drift objects were found off Greenland," the general said. "But it would seem more reasonable to trace them to another vessel, not the drift." The Pole could not be reached in a ship, he declared. "We know almost as well as if we had seen it, that there is in the unknown regions an extensive land which is the birthplace of the flat-topped iceberg. . . ."

Ignoring them, Nansen said he planned to put a ship into the ice near Siberia, where the *Jeannette* was lost. He stated flatly, as if he already had its plans in his head, that the ship must be especially constructed to take the ice, drift with it, and not be crushed by it as the *Jeannette* had been. That drift with the ice would take Nansen's dream ship across the Arctic, passing near the Pole, then the Greenland Current would carry her on the Atlantic side.

Before he did any more talking he accomplished two spectacular feats to prove to himself that he could handle arctic elements. On skis, during midwinter, he did what no other man had done. Alone, he crossed the rugged mountains between Oslo and Bergen.

Then, in 1888, with three other Norwegians and a Lapp, in seventy-five days, he skied across the great Greenland Ice Cap, traveling from the uninhabited east coast to the west, cutting off any possibility of retreat. That gave him some immediate international stature. It had taken planning, courage, and knowledge of how to handle oneself in the Arctic. On that Greenland expedition he collected drift ice caked with mud. Believing that it had to have broken free and drifted to Greenland from Siberia,

Nansen took the drift ice to a scientist, Dr. Tornebohm, who studied it and declared that he found twenty minerals in the drift mud. "This quantity of dissimilar constituent mineral parts," he said, "points to the fact that they take their origin from a very extensive tract of land, and one's thoughts naturally turn to Siberia."

That was it for Nansen. He committed himself to his theory and the Arctic.

The Arctic is an all-inclusive word taken from the Greek *arktos*, meaning the northern constellation, the Great Bear, and pertains to the land and the sea closest to the North Pole, the end of the earth's axis of rotation, which Nansen would discover to be nothing but formations of pack ice over great depths of water. Based on standard definitions, the Arctic itself includes regions consisting of the Canadian Archipelago, northern Alaska, all of Spitsbergen, Greenland, the eastern Arctic islands, northern Siberia, and the northern edge of Norway.

Nansen planned to go far beyond these known geographic positions. His Greenland ski episode had not only given him confidence, but gained him cooperation from some scientists. He continued to collect more evidence to prove the Siberian drift theory. Objects that could have originated only in Alaska, implements traced to Eskimos, and driftwood from trees common in Siberia continued to turn up on the shores of Greenland.

Although he had majored in zoology, Nansen was a born oceanographer, as were his uneducated Viking forebears who sailed the Arctic Ocean a thousand years ago. He pointed out that many rivers of North America and Asia flow into the Arctic Ocean. Rain and snow fall on that ocean. Nansen believed that this precipitation not only lowered the salt content of the water, but that that water must also have an outlet.

It had to be, he said, the channel between Spitsbergen and Greenland, where the strong East Greenland Current swept. No other place could carry the great flow of water. The currents in Bering Strait were weak, and the space between Iceland and Norway carried a northward current. Thus that volume of water in the East Greenland Current had to be the answer.

This water, Nansen speculated, must be gathered from distant sources. He was certain that the polar current reached to the coast of Siberia and drew from there.

After he had announced his theory, to the continued ridicule of foreign experts, he concentrated on planning the construction of a ship that would prove him right. He drew rough plans. Sides must slope so ice couldn't grasp it. That slope should also make the ship *rise* when caught between ice floes, not be pressed down and destroyed as the *Jeannette* had been. It had to be of reasonable size, yet large enough to comfortably sustain twelve men for as long as five years if they were trapped by the ice.

When Nansen submitted his plans to the Norwegian Geographic Society on February 18, 1890, he received its support and that of several wealthy businessmen. The Society advanced $55,000 to build Nansen's ship.

At the time Nansen was planning to drift to the North Pole region it was a feat comparable to that of Columbus discovering America. Many other explorers had tried and failed. American naval lieutenant Robert E. Peary had attempted it a dozen times and was still trying. There is evidence that it was Nansen's modesty, his scientific interests, and his philosophy that won him the support of his own countrymen.

He had more in mind than fame in reaching the North Pole. When he was twenty-three years old he said, "It is not to seek for the exact mathematical point that forms the northern extremity of the earth's axis that we set out, for to reach this point is intrinsically of small moment. Our object is to investigate the great unknown region that surrounds the pole."

The ship that would take him there, yet to be built, Nansen

called the *Fram*, Norwegian for "forward." As builder he selected Norway's most respected shipbuilder, the patriarchal-looking, gray-bearded Colin Archer, a fastidious craftsman.

Archer made many drawings and models before he and Nansen were satisfied. Then, with Nansen and Otto Sverdrup, who had crossed Greenland with Nansen and would be captain of the *Fram*, watching every step, it took three years to build the walnut-shaped ice ship that violated many building principles and was the first vessel of its kind ever constructed.

The *Fram*'s keel was made of two American elms, fourteen inches square, fifty-one feet long. The stem was built of three blocks of oak placed inside one another, four feet of solid oak. The ship was braced everywhere with iron rods and straps. The stern, also constructed of solid oak, had two wells that permitted the propeller and the rudder to be raised on deck for repairs.

The important ribbing was donated by the Norwegian Navy. Made of very special Italian oak, the ribs were grown in a curve and had been seasoned for thirty years.

A careful, ingenious man, Archer laid another hard skin of greenheart oak over the double oak planking, twenty-eight inches of solid, watertight wood, installed double-strength deck beams, a fore-and-aft sailing rig, an Akers triple-expansion, economical 220-horsepower steam engine. The crew's quarters were insulated with triple thicknesses and personally tested by Nansen.

He also realized what the constant lateral thrust of ice could do to a ship if the ship were subject to it for long periods. So he insisted that there should be many great bow timbers, several times the number that went into even the rugged herring sloops and sealers.

But then, Nansen had always been an original thinker. In his early twenties he broke with Norwegian custom that dictated that it was necessary to wear bulky woolen clothing. Nansen thought that clothing should allow free and effective body movement and wore neat, tailored pants and jackets and odd little hats. One member of the Geographic Society who met Nansen thought he was either a circus acrobat or an actor.

But by the time Nansen had organized the *Fram* expedition he was thirty-two years old and a completely dedicated man who would wear and do anything required to follow his dream to that unknown region farthest north. He was husky, over six feet tall, and kept himself in excellent physical condition by strenuous snowshoeing and skiing. His blond hair was thin and he had a rather innocuous wispy moustache. But his big frame and fierce eyes impressed those who first met him. He looks out at us from portraits of that time as a sober Viking of a man with a somewhat haunted expression in his pale, almost limpid eyes.

Tested periodically as it was being built, Nansen's *Fram* was launched in Oslo in the fall of 1892. It sailed on its own journey into silence on June 21, 1893. It had taken Nansen nine years to put his idea and his ship afloat.

With its rounded hull, the *Fram*, rigged as a three-masted fore-and-aft schooner, rolled heavily in the rough waters in the northern run along the Norway coast. All hands were seasick and concerned about the seaworthiness of the ship. But beyond North Cape the water became quieter and the *Fram* moved easily into the Kara' Sea and neared the New Siberian Islands. They didn't reach the point where the *Jeannette* had been mauled to death by pack ice. That same ice held the *Fram* back for over two months.

Reasoning that he might be gripped in ice and held to the coast for a full year, Nansen impetuously took the *Fram* directly north, and, using both sail and steam, pushed her into the central polar ice pack. Here, caught in what later was known as the Laptev Sea, the *Fram* began the long drift with the ice floes.

When the ship finally slid off the continental shelf Nansen began taking soundings. It was done by unraveling a steel cable and splicing the ends so there would be enough line to reach great depths. Nansen had thought that the polar sea would be shallow, with much of its water being made up of the transpolar current. That current, however, proved only part of the surface.

One depth they sounded was 12,600 feet. The experts then were wrong. With such depth there could be no continental land mass in this central region of the Arctic.

Now, with thirteen men and provisions for five years, the four-hundred-ton *Fram* was to drift in the grip of the ice for three years. The ice bullied them and almost broke them, even hurling itself on deck, but the *Fram* design proved fit, and the ship endured and defied the frozen giants in the sea that hammered at her.

The *Fram*, the pioneer, the first of the ice breakers, didn't get as close to the North Pole as Nansen had hoped, mainly because they hadn't been able to proceed far enough north before encountering the ice barrier in the autumn of 1893. The farthest north the *Fram* reached with Nansen aboard was latitude 85° 57′ N on October 16, 1895. (One degree of latitude equals sixty nautical miles. Since 90° N is the Pole, the point of 85° N would be about three hundred miles south of the Pole.) The *Fram* was unable to move farther north than this latitude because the sea ice that held it in its grip then began drifting south.

But Nansen decided to prove his point despite his ice-locked ship. He would leave the captain, Otto Sverdrup, and ten men to take the *Fram* on its drift; and, with one companion, Nansen would try to reach the Pole on foot.

No man had ever attempted it before, but Nansen had thought about it for months and was convinced that it could be done.

On March 14, 1895, Nansen and Hjalmar Johansen, a husky, strong army lieutenant in his early twenties who had signed on the *Fram* as a stoker so he could join the expedition, left the ship. Their plan: travel the shifting polar sea ice pack as far north as possible, exploring the unknown regions toward the Pole. Then return to Norway by sled and kayak through the Franz Josef Archipelago, a barren group of islands northeast of Spitsbergen.

Always a meticulous planner, Nansen spent weeks compiling a list of the equipment they would take on their march across the treacherous ice. Knowing that easily prepared, nutritious food was all important on sled trips, he had just muscle meat taken from an ox, freed it from fat and gristle, dried it quickly when fresh, then ground it and mixed it with ground beef suet. He brought fish flour, which was prepared as a dinner simply by heating in water and mixing with dried potatoes. He insisted that all food not need actual cooking, just warming. He also took two kayaks, one of which he designed and built himself.

A partial list of equipment included a pump (for pumping out kayaks in case of leakage); sail; ax and geological hammer; two guns, cases, and cartridges; theodolite and case; three reserve cross-pieces for sledges; harpoon and line; fur gaiters; five balls of cord; Finn shoes filled with grass; two pairs of kayak gloves; two waterproof sealskin kayak overcoats; one tent of undressed silk; one sack of "leverpostei," a pâté made of calf's liver; bag of sewing materials and medicines; petroleum lamp (primus); pocket flask; two oak staffs; one coil of rope; one double sleeping bag of reindeer calf skin; three Norwegian flags. In all about two thousand pounds of equipment that was to be pulled on three sleds by twenty-eight dogs and the two men.

For a few days it looked as if the idea of the march over the ice was a good one. As they moved north, the drifting sea ice seemed to smooth out, and they were making as much as fourteen miles a day.

But too soon the ice became razor-sharp high ridges and hummocks, clothing and equipment became heavy with moisture which quickly froze. "There is no possibility of drying or changing one's clothes," Nansen wrote. "And one must wear a chain mail of ice until they thaw in the sleeping bag and dry on the body."

They had to help the dogs pull the sleds, each carrying about eight hundred pounds, up over the icy ridges. Leads, open water, unexpectedly appeared. They could not go around them so they had to load everything into kayaks to cross the deep water, then reload into the sleds. Frostbite, biting cold, as low as sixty degrees below zero, the constant terrible lifting of the sleds slowed their progress to as little as three miles a day.

Nansen's eye was always on the purpose of his trip, and he was a precise and constant observer, keeping a diary, listing all the physical characteristics of the region, and, in the retreat south, detailing the animal tracks, the kind of bird life they saw. He did not overconcentrate on the physical discomfort, but once in exasperation wrote, "I tried to make it a rule that our marches were to be of nine or ten hours duration. In the middle of the day we generally had a rest and something to eat—as a rule bread and butter, with a little pemmican or liver pâté. These dinners were a bitter trial. We used to try and find a good sheltered place, and sometimes even rolled ourselves up in our blankets, but all the same the wind cut right through us as we sat on the sledges eating our meal. Sometimes, again, we spread the sleeping bag out on the ice, took our food with us, and crept well in, but even then did not succeed thawing either it or our clothes. When this was too much for us we walked up and down to keep ourselves warm, and ate our food as we walked. . . ."

They ran short of dog food. In a chore that became a horror for both men, the least efficient dogs had to be killed to feed the others. They couldn't waste ammunition on the job, so they cut the dog's throat. This became so bloody that they then tried strangulation. But that didn't work. They tied a rope around a dog's neck and each took hold of an end and tugged. But the dog survived. Some dogs refused to eat their own kind. These were scheduled for early execution. Nansen had nightmares about this terrible but necessary task.

Finally Nansen wrote, "The ice grew worse and worse. Yesterday it brought me to the verge of despair, and when we stopped this morning I had almost decided to turn back. I will go on one day longer, however, to see if the ice is really as bad farther northward as it appears to be from the ridge, thirty feet in height, where we are encamped. We hardly made four miles yesterday. Lanes, ridges, and endless rough ice, it looks like an endless moraine of ice blocks; and this continual lifting of the sledges over every irregularity is enough to tire out giants. Curious this rubble-ice. For the most part it is not so very massive, and seems as if it had been forced up somewhat recently, for it is incompletely covered with thin, loose snow, through which one falls suddenly up to one's middle. And thus it extends mile after mile northward—"

The next day, April 8, finding the ice rising in terrible ragged hills as they moved north, realizing that every day the ice on which they were traveling was drifting southward, Nansen gave it up and decided to head for land.

He had reached 86° 13'6" north, farther north than any man had ever gone.

Walking through shifting ice rubble and soft wet snow, and ice slush that sometimes came up to their chests, living on gulls, being trailed by polar bears (Johansen just missed death when one had him on his back and was about to bite his head but was distracted by a dog, then shot by Nansen), by August 14 they reached open water. They had killed their last two dogs. They lashed the kayaks together and, sailing the coast, after being attacked and nearly sunk by a giant, tusked walrus, finally reached a barren island in the Franz Josef Archipelago. They built a hut of stones, roofed it with their tent and spent nine months there, living on bears and seals that they shot. This was a bitter experience, the cold was intense, hope low.

During May 1896 they left the island, paddling the kayaks along the coast. They fought their way through the rough Arctic Ocean for a month. One day in early June they climbed out of the kayaks onto an ice floe to rest. To save labor, they had hoisted a small sail on the kayaks, still lashed together. They had just sat down on the floe when a wind suddenly sprang up, caught the sail on the kayaks and scooted them away.

Everything—food, clothing, all equipment, their lives—was in the kayaks. Without hesitation, Nansen jumped into the freezing water and swam after the kayaks. It has been scientifically recorded that seven to fifteen minutes in the Arctic Ocean this far north at this time of year brings unconsciousness, profound shock, and cardiac arrest.

Nansen was immediately numbed and cramped. He fought through the water until he could barely move his limbs. Then he turned on his back and weakly paddled.

He reached the boats, moving feebly now, stiff from cold and shock. Several times he tried to hook a leg up into the kayaks and failed. Finally, moving as if frozen in one piece without arms and legs, he made it and dragged himself in. Somehow he paddled to the floe where Johansen waited, first in horror, then in astonishment.

Working fast, Johansen got Nansen out of the boat, stripped, dried, and vigorously massaged him, then covered him with all the dry clothing and furs they had in the kayaks. He poured hot seal broth down his throat. That Nansen survived was a medical miracle accomplished by two factors: Nansen's strength and will and Johansen's fast action.

Afterward, Nansen wrote, "I was undeniably a good deal exhausted."

When Nansen regained his strength, they pushed on,

reaching Cape Flora on June 17. Resting shortly, they decided to strike off for Spitsbergen and ran into unbelievable luck. After paddling a few miles, they saw the ship of British explorer Frederick Jackson. Running the kayaks up to the bow, Nansen tipped his hat to the astonished Englishman and said, "How do you do?" Jackson took Nansen and Johansen aboard his ship, the *Windward*, and brought them to Norway.

In August the *Fram* finally escaped the clutch of the ice pack and broke into the open sea northwest of Spitsbergen. With Otto Sverdrup at the helm, it had drifted with the ice from September 25, 1893 until August 13, 1896.

Nansen became an immediate world celebrity. He had proved his theory about the drift of the transpolar current. He had discovered and explored the unknown North Polar Basin, with the proven conclusion that no land existed north of Spitsbergen, Franz Josef Land, the Eurasian Archipelagos, Taimir Peninsula, and the New Siberian Islands.

Nansen was also the first to bring back scientific data and personal observations on the biology of the polar sea, the formation of ice, the effect of wind on sea ice, the distribution and movement of ocean currents, the temperature, salinity, and depth of the unknown waters of the far north.

But Fridtjof Nansen was much more than a courageous explorer of the frozen wastes of the north. He was a scientist, a talented author, and a teacher. In 1897 he became professor of zoology at the University of Christiania and, in 1908, professor of the work he liked best and for which he had considerable talent, oceanography. He wrote six volumes, *The Norwegian North Polar Expedition 1893–1896*, which gave him substantial scientific status. He also continued exploring, went on another expedition to the Arctic Ocean in 1900, joined the expedition with the *Veslemøy* in 1912 to the unknown ocean north of Spitsbergen, and in 1913 mounted an expedition up Russia's Yenisei River.

The results of some of his research were published in *The Norwegian Sea, Its Physical Oceanography Based Upon the Norwegian Researches 1900–1906.*

Nansen also served with distinction as Norway's first Ambassador to England, from 1906 to 1908, but it was his compassion and devotion to humanitarian causes that added the greatest luster to his name, even outshining his courage.

In 1920 Nansen was made High Commissioner by the Council of the League of Nations, his duty to handle the repatriation of the prisoners-of-war from several countries who were still living in appalling conditions in prison camps throughout Europe. While engaged in this task, he was also asked to arrange for the rehabilitation of millions of displaced people and refugees, many of them White Russians, who were spread over Europe and Asia when World War I ended. At this time he created the Nansen Passport for the stateless, a document recognized by fifty nations. He set up large-scale relief for the people in the Ukraine and the Volga region of Russia, where famine and epidemics were widespread. In 1922, when the Greeks were defeated by the Turks, Nansen arranged relief for Greek refugees who had been living in Turkey, and organized exchange of the minority populations between Greece and Turkey. He was given the Nobel Peace Prize in 1922.

Some mighty men had passed through Tromsø.

4

Spouting smoke from her stacks, the *D/S Lyngen* lay at the dock like a sick, beached whale, her once steely gray hide scaling, flecked with rust. As I arrived she started an impatient hooting. Many of Tromsø's citizens were here to see her sail. People were pouring on and off the ship as if there were an emergency. Gulls flared over her like an unfurling fan.

That strange sun that defused the moon and burned out the stars spotlighted the midnight scene.

Men and women loaded with baggage were hustling aboard, dropping their bags on deck, then rushing off to get more gear or to help others. They wore raincoats, alpaca-lined jackets, heavy sweaters, arctic gear with hoods, some even city clothes.

Four stout women in heavy woolen suits and alpine hats with gay feathers in the bands strode up the gangplank like military police, erect, haughty. Bags in either hand, they boarded the ship with cold authority. I would remember these women well.

The local sightseers stood back making running comments

in Norwegian, chuckling and giggling at the flurry of activity.

These citizens, hemmed in by the Arctic, were always interested in going to the docks to size up those who were going even farther north. But tonight there was another reason: scientists from all over the world had gathered here to take the *Lyngen* to Longyearbyen.

I learned this from my usual informant, Wilhelm Bolin, who patiently talked with me about everything from Amundsen and Nansen to the virtues of the local museums. I should have recognized that the passengers were scientists. They must be the easiest professional group to identify, with a certain dreamy air, a lack of reality about schedule, or clearing the gangway, or getting aboard on time. A small group stood blocking progress, obviously discussing the gulls gyrating above the ship. Two bearded men in bright sweaters leaned against piers, deep in a conversation that had to be broken up by a seaman from the *Lyngen*, who went from person to person, tapping each on the shoulder, urging him aboard.

There were Africans, Asians, Europeans, North and South Americans, West Indians. I could hear Australian and New Zealand accents, conversations in French, Italian, and Spanish. It seemed more like the departure of the Orient Express from Istanbul than that of an old ship in northern Norway preparing to sail to the top of the world.

There was an air of excitement; people kept arriving jabbering to one another in their own language. A big, blond Norwegian stood at the dock entrance motioning newcomers toward the ship.

They had come from Stockholm, where the five Nordic countries—Denmark, Finland, Iceland, Norway, and Sweden—were hosting the International Geographical Congress. Four thousand delegates from sixty countries were attending.

The eighty or so boarding the *Lyngen* were going on a

special Spitsbergen excursion arranged by Norway, sailing as far as King's Bay, north of Longyearbyen. They were due to return for the opening of the Congress in Stockholm. I was lucky to find a berth on the crowded ship.

I had thought that a geographical congress would concentrate solely on geography. And so it does, I was told by a scientist whom I asked.

"But that geography," he said loftily, "includes the physical, biological, human, social, and economic phenomena around the globe in their complex, functional interrelations and in their regional differentiation." He looked hard at me. "That is why we need these international congresses. To share our findings and knowledge."

That self-conscious importance on the part of the scientists was largely relaxed as we pulled farther away from the shores of Tromsø. They were going into new, mainly uncharted country and the spirit of adventure soon was the order of the day. With such a collection of minds on board, it was a floating university.

Hooting, the *Lyngen* skillfully cleared the port, which was skittering with schooners, fishing smacks, sealers, big herring trawlers, and a miscellaneous fleet of smaller private craft. I was surprised at how soon we lost sight of the city and its harbor. It was as if it had sunk in the sea without a trace.

Leg number four under way. Steamship to Longyearbyen.

The *Lyngen* was an old lady. There were flaky rust spots on the deck, her lifeboats needed painting, smokestacks were smudged black, and she creaked as we went. The seamen were not shipshape, the captain was invisible, and his ship rode hard. But she was big and she looked rugged. A 120-foot steamship of five hundred tons with hand-fired coal boilers, she had been built in 1931, put into Arctic service in 1934, and spent the months of June, July, August, and September plying the waters from

Tromsø to Spitsbergen, going only as far north as King's Bay. But that was quite a haul, probably a week in waters that could be very rough.

The North Atlantic touched Tromsø, but as we left we sailed close to the Norwegian Sea and the Barents Sea, striking directly north, leaving the Atlantic behind. I had the idea that the *Lyngen* was a coastal steamer and that we would be traveling for some distance along some sort of coast. Actually, we did skirt the shoreline at first, but soon left coasts behind. And with a seemingly endless expanse of water ahead, I had the immediate feeling of being completely cut off from civilization. The feeling never left as the ship started across that blank space over which George Herz had run his finger as he sat at his desk. Even on his map the distance from Tromsø to my destination had seemed considerable, the islands of Svalbard floating forlorn and far away, the seas immense.

There was immediate camaraderie. Gulls followed us, flowing like a gigantic white banner above the ship. A tall, skinny man without a hat, his hair abundant but graying, stood beside me at the rail. He looked like a stork and actually was an ornithologist. I believe he was English and his name was Bunting.

"We will lose the treeline today," he said in a high, thin voice. "We're committed to the north. No more trees. The ice will start appearing soon."

The rail was full, men and women standing elbow to elbow from one end of the *Lyngen* to the other. The gulls mewed like cats over us.

Bunting looked up. "Mostly herring gulls. Hear that sound like a hundred pussy cats? That's gull for contentment."

"I thought they were one big gullet," I said, "that they were content only when eating."

He laughed, a stuttering sound. "Truth in that. But not

wholly. They're a bit more than a gullet. Remarkable, really. Gulls are about the only creatures that can drink salt water. Have a pair of big glands over their eyes that filter it."

He pointed at them high above us. "What single aspect do you get from that flock up there?"

Beauty. Grace. Trite words for gulls. "They're moving without flapping a wing."

"Good man!" Bunting said, pleased. "Their bones are hollow, weigh about one-seventh of their three pounds. Means they can get airborne instantly. But they're clever fellows, mind. With that five-foot wingspan, the way they hold their feet back to reduce air drag, they can use any current. Right now, as you observed, they are not working to fly. The ship is producing thermals, a current of air. Gulls will stay with us as long as they can use that thermal. So it isn't true that they follow ships just for handouts. They do certainly. But that isn't the only reason."

Word ran along the rail that we would be stopping at a small island, Hornsund, where a group of Polish scientists had established a meteorological station.

The second day out of Tromsø the ice did appear, and even my inexperienced eye could see that there was a difference in the flat ice and the other barrel-sized, cubelike pieces that caught the fire of the sun. I hoped that I would meet a man aboard who knew as much about ice as Bunting did about birds.

The *Lyngen* made no effort to avoid the ice, its bulk gave it right of way. The captain knew these waters and would be aware of any ice large enough to bypass. She wouldn't actually dodge the ice, *Lyngen* was too large a ship for that. But before long we began encountering ice that the captain maneuvered around in a precise, stately fashion. Some floes the size of lifeboats were streaked with rose and violet, the sun burning in the ice like a lamp. We struck one and there was a crunching like the grinding of glass.

Our first view of Svalbard would be of Bear Island, the one that Barents, the Dutch explorer, had named in 1596. We had been told that the island would probably be banked in fog.

It was, but not completely. We could see cliffs standing like palisades.

Bjørnøya, as the Norwegians call Bear Island, is historic because it was the first of the Svalbard Islands to be discovered. The *Lyngen* cut her engines while we watched hundreds of auks, guillemots, and various species of gulls in a continuous spurt above the high cliffs lifting straight out of the sea. A radio and meteorological station was there and I wondered if any of the passengers on the polar flights knew that their way was charted by men in these incredibly lonely stations.

A scientist with binoculars at the rail beside me reported that he thought he saw the rusted rails of a narrow-gauge railroad and large white skeletons. "Whales and walrus," another man at the rail said. "They once used Bear Island as a whaling center."

While we stared at the barren place rising as starkly out of the sea as a great reptile, seamen were busy with hand lines. Norwegians will cast a line whenever they get the opportunity. The Bjørnøya fishing banks were famous—sometimes fifty pounds of cod were hauled in in less than an hour. About a dozen silvery fat fish were yanked aboard before the *Lyngen* got under way again.

Now we were getting constant sounds of ice cracking against the bow of the *Lyngen*, and the water here along the coasts of Svalbard stayed rough. We walked the deck with difficulty and hung on to the rail with both hands.

The first view of Hornsund was of floating mountain peaks. In the distance, the broken coast of this archipelago in the Arctic Ocean stretched ahead like a solid wall of ice-covered rock.

Hornsund seemed pressed to the sea by mountains of ice. Directly to its north the Torell glacier stuck its giant icy tongue between two mountains looking as if it would split them asunder.

As we approached the island we could see that for some distance inland it was clear of snow and ice. The master of the *Lyngen* apparently had been in radio contact with Hornsund, for as we hove to in the little bay before the island, a small motorboat came out to meet us.

Beyond Hornsund reared mountains capped in snow. Cloud and mist hung over them, but did not obscure the ice cap far beyond the mountains, streaked in blue, flaring when struck by the sun.

Our visitor from shore was the leader of the Polish scientists, a regal old man with a full white beard. He bowed and paid his respects to the captain and the ship's officers and met the prominent scientists aboard, inviting all the scientists to visit his meteorological station.

I climbed into one of the boats going ashore, to visit the small station, full of complicated-looking radio and weather equipment. Although the closest mountains were dusted with snow, the open area and hills near the station were free of ice and snow. Our scientists weren't too interested in the observation station itself; they scampered around the island like excited children at a playground, getting samples of rock, shale, lichen, bird feathers, vegetation. Some of them were busy with notebooks and pencils, others with magnifying glasses.

We spent two hours ashore, the scientists bringing their findings back to the *Lyngen* with them. The dozen Poles joined us aboard for dinner, the scientists sitting in small groups at individual tables chatting animatedly. There were several small dining rooms set up to handle about one hundred passengers.

On board an old rough-riding ship sailing Arctic water, breakfast, lunch, and dinner can assume proportions out of their ordinary dimension. With me mealtime also became a marathon.

Those four stout women in wool suits I had noticed

marching aboard the *Lyngen* in Tromsø proved to be German biologists. They spoke no English, and did not have manners in any language. When they came upon a small group of people talking they did not detour but plowed straight through. On deck they confiscated the sunniest spots away from the wind and stood basking like great fat cats. But it was at breakfast and dinner when they became real storm troopers.

Meals were served from a central buffet table, with everyone making his own selection. That sounds cozy, but actually it became a near desperate competition trying to get to that table before the quartet of fraus. I never made it. They formed a phalanx, moving around the circular table shoulder to shoulder, making it impossible for anyone else to touch the food until they had made their deliberate choice, heaping their plates with the best of everything.

We hadn't been at sea more than a day when the rough water let us know that we were remote from the well-traveled sea lanes. When the ship began pitching, all dining tables had their cloths liberally sprinkled with water to keep plates from sliding off. During these times the dining room was nearly deserted. Rough seas do not build an appetite. But no matter how rough it got, the four women were always at that buffet table when the ship's bell tolled time to dine.

One day, when scarcely a dozen passengers stirred from their closetlike cabins, every plate in the dining room nearest my cabin crashed to the deck in a thunderous sound that brought running the few of us who were able to get out of our bunks, thinking we had hit an iceberg.

There in the dining room were the four stalwarts, complaining bitterly to the waitresses about the spilled food and their breakfast being disturbed.

My stomach heaved and the man beside me grew pale at the sight. Food was splashed about everywhere, plates, cups and saucers were shattered. The sight and smell upset me so much that I couldn't visit the dining room for some time.

As I left, nausea rising, the four biologists were returning to their table, clean plates reasonably well filled.

But despite rough water and the greedy four, during those four and a half days on the *Lyngen*, I received a liberal education in Norwegian food.

Having eaten in restaurants in Oslo and Bergen, I thought I knew something about the country's cuisine. But restaurants tend to serve what they think will appeal to tourists, labeling it "continental." I had eaten the spectacular Norwegian *smørgåsbord*, a buffet spread with seafood delicacies, tiny shrimps, lobsters, crab, smoked eel, fish of all kinds, and I thought that the Norwegian *hummer*, lobster, smaller than ours, was the best that I had ever eaten. I also knew their *østers*, very small but sweet and delicious oysters. Their partridge, *ryper i fløtesaus*, a whole ptarmigan in a rich cream, served with lingonberries, was superb. So were *multer*, cloudberries, yellow berries picked high in the mountains and served very ripe with whipped cream.

But that was fancy landlubber food. The *Lyngen* believed in the basics.

There were four waitresses, middle-aged, dour, uncommunicative women who seemed to get absolutely no joy out of life, and surely none out of their jobs. They did no waiting on table. They cleared them, but brought no food. At our first meal not too long after we sailed out of Tromsø, one hefty dark-haired waitress with a hard face but lively brown eyes that moved everywhere except in your direction when she talked, said, "Your napkin. Only one you get for the voyage. Take care of it." With that she slapped it on the table in an envelope. It was a large linen napkin, and the waitress meant what she said. It was indeed the only napkin, and by the end of the trip looked like a relief map of Norway.

All food was placed on that large aforementioned buffet table. *Frokost,* breakfast, was always *koldtbord,* a cold table, and took some getting used to. I did manage to get some hot tea, but my stomach continued to jump whenever I took it up to that cold table early in the morning. Fish was always in great array, little brisling sardines, *sild,* herring, the national dish in at least twenty varieties, and in some places in Norway over one hundred. The *Lyngen* was famous, or infamous, depending upon your point of view, for its *sursild,* herring filets cured in brine, served cold with raw onion rings, and occasionally with hot boiled potatoes. There were several cheeses; the best, *jarlsberg,* looked like Swiss but had more character and a nutty flavor. There also were Norwegian goudas, tilsit, edam, and blue, very creamy, and a *taffelost,* a sour-tasting cheese that you almost got used to. But obviously the favorite of the ship's chef, one served every morning, was *gjetost,* made from boiled goat's milk, looking like brown laundry soap. With not quite the taste of soap, it was sweetish, the favorite Norwegian breakfast cheese. There was no toast for breakfast, but plenty of *flatbrød,* very thin, crackerlike rye bread.

But the Norwegians knew what they were doing. On days when the water was so rough that the ship rolled like a bathtub and the stomach was a most delicate object that had to be pampered, the only thing it could handle was bread and cheese. I quickly learned a lesson that I would remember and use on the *Havella,* in water that made the rough spots that we navigated on the *Lyngen* seem like a millpond.

There was no *lunsj,* lunch, but there was a *middag,* dinner, served anytime from noon to three P.M., and usually we did have an *aftens,* supper, some kind of cold meat sandwich and a hot drink. Once we had a sort of surprise for this meal, *benløse fugler,* toughish slices of cold boiled beef tied together with string to somewhat resemble a bird and stuffed with big lumps of beef fat.

So the *Lyngen* was far removed from a cruise ship. Four

French scientists had a very bad time at every meal, picking sparingly and superciliously from the *koldtbord*. I noticed for their first breakfast they had only flatbread and cheese, but by the time we were ready to disembark they had worked up to two kinds of fish.

Middag was noted for its *akevitt,* or aquavit, a most potent white liquor (sometimes called "scalp-lifter") distilled from potatoes and flavored with caraway seeds. Norway's national drink, it was always served with meals and chased with *øl,* beer. On the *Lyngen,* the beer was a *pils,* a light lager type.

We also had a little variety at dinner. No epicure will dispute that Norwegian salmon is the world's best. We had it once poached, *kokt laks,* with a creamy white sauce and tiny parsley-speckled boiled potatoes. We also had the famous *fårikål,* mutton and cabbage stew, liberally seasoned with black pepper and served with boiled potatoes. There was another stew, *lapskaus,* chewy beef with potato cubes in thick brown gravy.

Although I am not a breakfast man, usually settling for tea and toast with a little jelly, I began to approach that morning *koldtbord* with dragging step, and little montages of pink ham and eggs sunny side up, savory sausage, and crusty scrapple sizzling in the pan began appearing. As I nibbled at a cold herring at eight o'clock in the morning I remembered Wilhelm Bolin saying that the cook on the ketch, the *Havella,* was very good. As herring was followed by cheese I kept throwing that memory out like a life preserver to a drowning man.

There really wasn't all that concentration on food. Recollection sometimes builds a bit too grandly. There were interesting people aboard and much to think about on the journey ahead. But don't ever let anyone tell you that adventure, like an army, doesn't travel on its stomach.

It was simple luck, like falling down a mountain and being rescued by Sir Edmund Hillary (the man who climbed Mt.

Everest), meeting the one man on the *Lyngen* who probably knew most about glaciers. Toward the end of the second day out I was standing on deck watching ice bob in cold gray water. It was flat, pocked, brittle-looking ice. A man stood six feet from me, slender even in heavy tweeds. "Floes," he said. "Don't chop ice for your martini from those. Pure salt."

In an easy conversational tone, as natural as if he were discussing the weather, he chatted about the difference between icebergs and ice floes. Floes are formed by the surface of the sea freezing. Icebergs are frozen from fresh water inland before they reach the sea. He also explained that ice floes that float so innocently out there often break into jagged pieces covering a square mile or more, forming what is called pack ice. "Some ships have been imprisoned in it for months, even years."

"Nansen," I said.

He smiled indulgently. "And his follower, Amundsen."

Sensing that he was an expert, I said I was sorry to be so dense about this ice business and wondered if icebergs came from glaciers. I didn't tell him then, but I wasn't even sure I knew what a glacier was.

He was patient. "Sure. When either a glacier or part of an ice sheet reaches the sea without entirely melting, it rides on the sea floor until there is enough depth of water to float it. It then continues to move, pushed by the ice behind it, becoming thinner and thinner as it gradually melts. When it is only a few hundred feet thick, pieces often break off from the front edge—calving, this is called—and float away as icebergs. These so-called calves are more massive than they appear. You can see only the one-ninth portion that is above the water level. Submerged and large they are very dangerous. You will remember the *Titanic*."

He went on to tell me that some icebergs jut five hundred feet out of the water, and that one fifty miles long had been seen. They drift with the current, often traveling hundreds of miles in the cold polar water before they reach warmer currents and melt.

"Just from Greenland alone," he said, "ten thousand icebergs break away every year."

His voice was the soft, modulated one of the upper-middle-class Englishman. We introduced ourselves. He was R. Kay Gresswell, M.A., F.R.S.A., F.R.G.S., F.G.S., lecturer in Geomorphology at the University of Liverpool, and the author of *The Physical Geography of Glaciers and Glaciation*.

I learned all these credentials later. Our first meeting was a relaxed one. The ice conversation was resumed when I told him who I was and where I was bound, not wanting any misunderstanding about my status on this ship full of scientists.

I did not, however, tell R. Kay Gresswell my real reason for being aboard the *Lyngen*. I did not impetuously pour out that I was a sort of pilgrim making my way to Mecca, a mecca where no man had been for twelve years, a place where I hoped to find not only pure, untouched silence, but maybe even pieces of myself that would help me in placing a complicated world into perspective. I instinctively felt he would be a man I could talk with of such thoughts, but I was selfishly guarding any reference to such a rare place as the lost lake. Ostensibly I was going to Svalbard to study polar bears and to see the last wilderness of its kind left in our world.

"You're the lucky one," Gresswell said. "We're only going as far as King's Bay, this region's last outpost, then we must go back to Stockholm." He gave me a speculative look. "You're going to see some of the most spectacular country left."

He, of course, being an ice expert, was prejudiced.

"Those islands of Svalbard where you'll be going, and even the sea bottom around them were once ice sheets. The fjords and valleys, although they were river valleys, have all been shaped by glaciers."

He took off his tweed cap and ran fingers through his hair.

He was handsome, with even features and sparkling gray eyes. "I'm not exaggerating when I say that conditions on Svalbard's islands are exactly the same today as they were ten thousand years ago."

He said that some of the islands were completely covered with ice. Kvitøya's entire surface was ice; Nordaustlandet was half ice-sheeted, and the central area of Spitsbergen was solid ice, some of it more than two thousand feet deep.

The professor thought that there were more glaciers in Svalbard than any place on earth, that only the very small islands were without them. "The frozen crust in Svalbard is nine hundred feet deep," he said. "Even in warmest summer, such as we are now having, only one to three feet of surface thaws."

I must have shown my concern, for he quickly added, "But this time of year there are large areas free of ice and snow and you'll see some lovely arctic flowers. Broad valleys extend miles into the interior of Spitsbergen island, and if you walk to the end of a valley you'll see the receding tip of a glacier, which in its retreat probably has created small lakes, rivers, streams."

Over a *koldtbord* breakfast, at *middag,* and while just sitting and sipping aquavit, we talked about glaciers until I had a fair knowledge of those massive hunks of solid ice that had shaped our world.

I learned that there are eight hundred thousand square miles of land covered by ice in the Arctic, with two million square miles of polar cap ice in the Arctic Ocean, and ice cover of five million square miles in Antarctica.

Before we reached Longyearbyen, when I saw the sun glinting, sending rosy sparks off those ice monsters far off across the water, I knew that a glacier is a mass of compacted ice that originates in a snowfield and persists for many years. Glaciers form in areas where more snow falls than melts, in high mountains or polar regions. As the fall of snow accumulates, it is compressed into ice. This compacted snow and ice moves, because of its weight; downhill, if on a grade, or in several directions from its center, if it has formed on flat terrain. This glacial ice moves from a region of excess accumulation of snow to areas where the annual melt is higher than the snowfall.

I had some trouble grasping exactly how a glacier moved. Kay Gresswell, making me wish that I had the opportunity to sit in on all of his lectures in Liverpool, simply and patiently cleared it up.

Glacial ice flows down a mountainside the way a stream of water does, but much more slowly. Pressures begin within the ice on the downhill movement when the glacier approaches a bend or a narrow section in a valley. These pressures then cause temporary thawing of thin films within the glacier, so that the ice on two sides of the thaw can slide on itself, acting as though it is no longer one solid piece. When the pressure of bending is removed, the ice freezes solidly together again.

This so-called "moving by melting," known as regelation, can be compared with the action created by a person sliding or skating on ice. The pressure of his weight is sufficient to melt the ice beneath him without actually raising its temperature. The pressure produces a thin film of water between his feet or ice skates and the ice. This in turn acts as a lubricant enabling him to glide along. The thin film of water freezes again as soon as he removes pressure from it.

Glacial ice two hundred feet or more beneath the surface is not the brittle ice that we know. At that depth the ice becomes plastic, flexible. In this form it is able to almost "flow" like a river. However, unlike a river, the glacier's stiffness and pressure from the bulk of weight behind it as it moves downhill even enables it to move uphill for short distances.

That ice-pushing pressure from behind acts much like a line of freight cars being moved by an engine from the rear, pushing instead of pulling. Physical evidences at Loch Ness, Scotland, show that a glacier rode up over rock barriers three hundred feet high.

One time Kay Gresswell showed what a masterful teacher he was by taking advantage of some aquavit I spilled on a table when the *Lyngen* bucked and heaved, as she did more often than not.

"That great glacier which may cover many square miles moves out from its place of birth the very way that firewater you spilled is moving. It spreads in the same ever-widening circle on the flat surface. Weight at the center forces the edges outward. But the rate of movement varies. The center of a glacier moves faster than its sides or bottom because the bottom is slowed by rubbing against rocks and the earth's floor. Some glaciers, depending upon location, move a few inches a year, a very few move a hundred feet a week, but on the whole the movement averages out to about a foot a day. The great ice sheet covering many miles moves only a few feet a year, its center hardly at all."

Where do they end when they move?

Gresswell lit his pipe and blew a cloud of smoke at me. "You're the busiest brain picker I've ever met. I'm going to throw a fee at you before this bloody cruise is over."

But it didn't take a great brain to know that he enjoyed talking glaciers. When a professional is on his specialty the pleasure works both ways.

Glaciers end their movement where the rate of ice flow balances the rate of ice melt, or the rate of calving into the sea.

There are four types of glacier, apart from the vast polar ice sheets, which are a force and Ice Age unto themselves.

The Alpine, or long, thick valley glacier. The Piedmont, which is mostly Alaskan, and which can be described as valley glaciers joining to form an enormous sheet of almost stagnant ice. Third is the Greenland glacier, which has neither of the valley forms, and consists of an ice sheet covering much of the country and slopes toward the coast at a very low angle. When this ice reaches the coast it forms dramatic, solid, vertical or overhanging cliffs which are called Chinese Wall Front glaciers, prolific ones, calving frequently into the sea.

"The fourth," said the English professor, "is your very own special glacier, the Spitsbergen glacier."

This is a central ice cap on a high plateau, the sides deeply cut by valleys containing valley glaciers. These valley glaciers, off-shooting from the ice cap, often also form Chinese Wall Fronts when they reach the sea.

Being erudite, and having not only an interested but a captive audience of one, Gresswell also dropped some statistics and history. About three-fourths of the world's fresh water (equal to nearly sixty years of snow and rainfall over the earth) is frozen in glacial ice. In North America alone the amount of water locked in glaciers is far greater than in all rivers, lakes, ponds, and reservoirs.

The Ice Age lasted about one million years and ended only twenty thousand years ago. "Just ten thousand years ago," Gresswell said, "the city where I am going, Stockholm, was covered with ice."

He said that scientists weren't sure what caused the Pleistocene Glacial epoch, but while it lasted, in three stages, the ice went as far south as our Ohio Valley, and as far south in Europe as Bavaria. Right now about 5,800,000 square miles (or 10.4 percent of the land area of the world) are covered by glacial ice. Ninety-eight percent of this is in the Antarctic and the Arctic. During the Ice Age, ice covered a little more than 28 percent of the earth, only three times the area iced in today.

"Except where you are going," Gresswell said. "Fifty percent of Svalbard is a glacial mass. You are traveling backward in time to the Ice Age itself."

5

Longyearbyen looked even more desolate than I had pictured Gresswell's Ice Age. It was the contrast, man against mountain, mediocrity against majesty of sea, ice, and snowy peaks. The settlement seemed to be sitting there on the edge of the world, about to slide off.

All that had come before—the flight to Denmark, the prop plane to Norway, the bus to Tromsø, the *Lyngen* coughing smoke and rattling her bones as she trudged through lonely northern waters, even Hornsund, and the Poles at their desolate station, or that first close look at Svalbard—didn't give a true indication of how far we were really going. How far away from the world. None of it had the stark reality, the sense of utter futility, that was contained in my first look at man's puny efforts to establish himself in the wilderness here at Longyearbyen.

Now, as the old ship hove to at four P.M. on the fifth day out of Tromsø, her anchor chains clanking as they were being readied, and I could see all of Longyearbyen lying before me, a scattering of old clapboard buildings pitifully inadequate and forlorn against the bleak background of towering black mountains, I had two immediate reactions. I wanted to stay aboard the ship. And I wondered whether this was adventure or misadventure that I was getting myself into.

I had never seen black mountains. These loomed ominously. For a moment, the sight of this frontier settlement held everyone aboard silent, but scientists full of knowledge cannot remain silent long. It is a sacrilege they have sworn a blood oath not to commit.

It was a Dane, I believe, if memory can be depended upon, who began expounding upon the physical features of what we were seeing as the *Lyngen* came hooting into the harbor.

"Advent Bay," he said, "always ice-free this time of year. We are coming in on the west side of Adventfjord. That layer-cake mountain away in the distance with the flat top is Temple Mountain. Look beyond the buildings, that is Longyear Valley. At the top is Longyear Glacier, to its left is Lars Glacier. See how the two glaciers are separated by a spur of mountain called Sarcophagus."

He went on, pointing out a large building as the Governor's residence, the radio station with its many masts, and beyond another mountain, Mount Nordenskiold. "Over 3,500 feet high," he said. "And today we're in luck. It's usually shrouded in mist."

The mountain was crowned with snow, and long arms of ice stretched down its sides. Tall as it was, you could still see the glitter of the giants beyond, the big breeders of glaciers to the north, the ice caps.

A chill wind came off them, stirring a smell of coal dust and codfish. Two old fishing trawlers moved in the swell, split cod was drying on decks, and already three trucks heaped with coal were lining up to service the *Lyngen*. Before we docked it began to rain, a slanting gray curtain obscuring the view beyond the harbor.

Three of the African delegates to the International Geographical Congress stood beside me as the ship maneuvered into docking position, something akin to horror on their faces as they stared at the "capital of Svalbard."

They were dressed in long, alpaca-lined coats and black astrakhan hats. Two were slender, with soft brown eyes that moved like birds in a cage; the third, heavy-set, jolly, had a tribal slash on each cheek and a pronounced English accent probably nurtured at Oxford.

One said five explosive words in his own language; one said nothing, his eyes riveted to the mountains; the one with the scars turned to me and said, "Black mountains! How long do we stay *here?*"

"A special luncheon for you, I hear," I said. "That coal there on the trucks is going to be loaded, then I understand that you'll be on your way to King's Bay."

The African closed his eyes. "God bless."

I never did discover what sinister symbol black mountains held for them, for suddenly the Longyearbyen official greeters arrived in three cars. They took the most important of the scientists—who they were I never discovered—and the rest of them walked through the rain.

It was four hours before the *Havella* was due to arrive, so I went along to the luncheon that the Governor of Svalbard was giving for the delegates to the International Congress. I hadn't been singled out as not being one of the scientists and I just walked with them through the rain past a cluster of weathered houses, mine buildings, a tiny post office, a miners' canteen, a small hospital, a large mess hall, two workshops, and a power station.

One of the scientists asked a man standing near the power station where the luncheon was being given for the Congress. He grinned sourly and pointed. "You'll see the cars at the Community Center. No chance of getting lost here."

It was a barren place, lost in the shadows of the basalt mountains. We walked past seven cows that looked as strange as unicorns as they cropped anemic grass that would never have the time free from snow and ice to get green. Tiny white flowers struggled between rocks. Large white gulls swooped over our heads crying coarsely. Where was Bunting? What species were these monsters?

"That must be it," one scientist said, pointing to a large barnlike building. I knew some of these learned men's names, but there were too many for me to keep them straight. Gresswell and Bunting and a couple of others were conspicuous because of the information they had passed on to me.

I heard one of the scientists say that he understood about one thousand people lived here year around and that the Community Center was modern, with a cinema, a restaurant, a school, a church, chaplain's quarters, and several large rooms used for community functions including dances.

The Miners' Community Center had been built that year, undoubtedly at considerable cost, as it was constructed of wood and there were no trees for many miles, a fact of which I was painfully aware. As we entered, I could smell the resin of new lumber and the penetrating odor of wax. It was a huge raftered room, reminding me of the big Munich beer halls, especially when they began bringing in bottles of beer to go with the aquavit, and it had the same cheery atmosphere, everyone chattering and relaxed now that they were off the heaving old *Lyngen*, and had their feet on solid oak floor.

Trestle tables were set up along the perimeter of the room, and there was a head table set apart at the far end where the Norwegian in charge of the group of visiting scientists sat, as did the Governor, the captain of the *Lyngen*, the settlement's chaplain, the doctor, and others of note.

The four German biologists sat at a table with three men who already looked intimidated.

The Governor made a little speech in English, as did the Norwegian representing the group, both remarking how honored they were to have such a distinguished gathering here in Norway's most unique area.

The Governor told us that he was known as the Sysselmann, and that there was a Bergmester who was Commissioner of Mines, and a mines labor inspector, all of whom he introduced. He explained that his administration was subordinate to the Ministry of Justice, the Ministry of Industry, and the Ministry of Labor.

Remarking that Svalbard was only ten degrees south of the North Pole and farther north than the northernmost point of Alaska, he named the twelve major islands, Spitsbergen (where we now were), Nordaustlandet, Edgeøya, Barentsøya, Prins Karls Forland, Kong Karls Land, Kvitøya, Bjørnøya, Lågøya, Hopen, Danskøya, Storøya, and several lesser islands, such as the two we had seen, Bear and Hornsund.

"It's pretty big," the Governor said. "We are larger than Denmark, Switzerland, or Holland."

A big, bold-looking man, the Sysselmann added wryly, "But these islands are wild, rugged mountains. I oversee a vast wilderness. In their interiors large areas are ice-covered, and glaciers run down between sharp ridges and peaks to the larger valleys and the coastal lowland or right into the sea. These glaciers that calve into the sea keep the waters in an uproar with great splashings and thunderous noises that echo among the mountains. Both the west and north coasts are deeply indented by many large fjords."

Pointing out that, despite its isolation, Svalbard did have strategic value, he explained that the archipelago occupies a pivotal position for all sea traffic from Murmansk, Russia's major naval port in the White Sea. This traffic must pass between Svalbard and the Norwegian Capes before entering the Atlantic. The lonely weather stations on a few of the islands are important to all planes and ships operating in the Arctic. He added, a little tightly, I thought, that it was also believed that Svalbard could be tapped for oil.

He spoke amusingly of the trouble Norway had claiming sovereignty of Svalbard, with American, British, Swedish, Dutch, German, and Russian interests complicating the treaty. Three conferences were held without any agreement, until finally thirty-six powers granted Norway sovereignty in an agreement reached in Paris in 1920. Claims on Svalbard land staked before the treaty had to be negotiated. The result was that, of these properties, today 94 percent are Norwegian and four are Russian.

Then he went into the reason for Longyearbyen's existence and talked coal, explaining that the mines here, the world's most northerly, were discovered by American John Longyear of Boston, who sank the first shaft in 1905. Longyear thereby initiated a rush for mining rights, with Russia, Norway, and Sweden claiming Spitsbergen, the island where Longyearbyen was located.

Before the treaty, the coal in Svalbard belonged to anyone who mined it. In 1916 a Norwegian company, Store Norske Kulkompani A. S., bought the Longyearbyen mines from John Longyear.

Today, there is one Russian company, Arktik Ugol, mining coal. From 1907 through 1970, 24 million tons were exported from Svalbard, 14 million from Norwegian mines. "Presently," the Governor said proudly, "six hundred and fifty men take out half a million tons every year."

With that he sat down to a splatter of applause from the guests.

The Bergmester got a big hand when he arose, asked that more aquavit be poured, and said how pleased everyone at Longyearbyen was to welcome the visitors.

"All we see in summer are coal barges. In winter we see each other. We thank you for coming. It is encouraging to us to realize that there really is another world out there."

Scalp-lifters were held high and skoaled in toasts and a few scientists got to their feet and talked briefly about what they hoped to see here in Spitsbergen before they went back to Stockholm.

Then luncheon was served, the first in five days for everyone from the *Lyngen*. I saw expressions of relief on several faces, especially the Frenchmen, as this normal routine was again observed.

It was a singular Norwegian treat, *rensdyrstek,* reindeer steak served with rich brown gravy. It was tender, slightly sweet meat, and delicious. There weren't varieties of fish served first, as is the custom; the chef or perhaps the Governor seemed to have been aware that fish had been eaten in quantity all the way up from Tromsø.

After lunch there was a tour of the coal mines. I was surprised that few of the scientists were interested. Probably the others had seen coal mines before, but I hadn't, and I had always wondered about those deep dark caverns where men risked their lives every day. Afterward I was sorry that I had gone. It is a humiliating experience to learn that in this age men still work like medieval slaves. I still have bad dreams of crawling through a black mountain on my stomach, the sides of the caves closing in.

A truck took us up to one mountain mine. It was still raining, the cold, gray drizzle now mixing with spits of snow. In late July! It reminded me of where I was. The sun that never set was still trying to burn through, blurred, hazy. Below, the bay looked like the lake in New York's Central Park with children's toy boats floating on it.

The driver let us off at the top of the mountain, and I thought: You are going "up" to a coal mine not "down" and you are going to walk "through" a mountain not "over" it.

As we stepped through the opening of the mine, the brow of the mountain towering above us, I knew that I was going into the first aboriginal mountain I had ever seen, one that had to be at least five thousand million years old. Inside it was pitch black, the floor was frozen solid, and you had to walk very carefully. We entered the main gallery, which extended horizontal offshoots into the mountain. All the galleries were propped with heavy timber to keep rock from collapsing and blocking the exits.

We wore headlamps on light metal helmets and moved cautiously through the black heart of the mountain, hunching under props and rock overhang.

A miner was our guide, a huge young man in his twenties with long, coal-dusted yellow hair hanging beneath his helmet. He took us to a "stope," a mining term used to describe a certain type of excavation that had to be worked by men lying on their stomachs. A miner was using a long narrow electric saw, cutting away the lower section of a slab of coal. Coal dust flew; his face was black in seconds.

Yards away another miner, also flat on his stomach, was drilling a hole for an explosive charge.

The air seemed quite good, but it was cold, 27 degrees. It remained about that, even in winter, when it was 60 below outside. Miners were on their bellies like burrowing animals all around us. It was raining coal dust on the sides of the narrow gallery we were traveling. Our guide went before us spreading lime to bind the dust. It would also prevent explosions caused by pit gas.

It was damp; the cold came up from the floor as if by

ventilator. Even in the vaunted Grenfell coat I was shivering. There was utter silence in some of the galleries, in others you could hear the saws chewing away like giant rats. I fought claustrophobia as we went through the narrow passageways, our lights making pathetic little spots on the rough walls of the mountain. The smell of raw lime mingled with that of the fine, penetrating coal dust, making us cough, the sounds reverberating eerily. We were deep in the mountain and I followed the miner ahead closely. He was the lifeline, the way out. I questioned the wisdom of coming into this mine, wishing I had more contentment and less curiosity in my makeup.

I remembered reading that in many mines they released skunk scent in the shafts to quickly and silently warn the miners of danger, a signal for them to get out. I remembered that often entire sections simply collapsed without warning, burying the miners. I summoned will and shut off those thoughts. We had been assured that these mines were very nearly accident-proof. Our guide stopped, waiting for us to catch up with him, and I delayed the push deeper into the mine by asking questions. How long did they stay? What kept them here?

The miners spent three years before they were given leaves. He also told us of some of the compensations. Wages were high (how high he didn't say); income tax was only 4 percent, so they could save most of their salaries; a bottle of fine French wine, which cost fourteen shillings in Oslo, was only two shillings here. There was no tax on cigarettes and alcohol. He said the miners counted their time by winters, not by years. Getting through the sunless months after the constant darkness of their hours in the mountain mines was considered a major accomplishment.

We stopped at one stope where a miner was raking out coal that he had cut up with a saw. Lights from their headlamps flashing on one another's faces, the two miners talked animatedly in Norwegian for a while, both laughing. On the way out our guide told us that the other miner was finishing up his three years this week and was going on a three-month vacation to Paris.

"I was telling him what to do when he got there," the guide said, grinning. "He's got no experience and the French are peculiar people. Specially the girls."

Out of the mine I stood on the mountainside blinking. The light was intense after the darkness of the caverns. Coal dust was deep in my nostrils. I was relieved and grateful to be outside. Below in the bay the codfishing craft were moving out and coal colliers were coming in. Beyond them a sleek white ship skimmed across the water as gracefully as a gull. Could it be the *Havella* arriving? She was white.

For many days afterward I was haunted by the sight of those young miners digging into the bowels of the mountain. Eight hours a day for three years. It would be a long time before I complained about anything.

It had stopped raining. The truck was not there, so we walked about a mile to the mine buildings and I caught a ride to the quay.

The white ship I had seen swooping into the bay rode at anchor like a great sea bird. It was the *Havella*, living up to her name, Sea Duck.

6

I believe I would have recognized her even before I saw her name. She moved gently in the swell, so elegant that, in contrast, the sturdy gray coal colliers around her looked like flotsam and jetsam. With her long, clean lines she resembled the motor-sailors of Long Island Sound—with an important difference, as I knew from Bolin. Back in Tromsø he had answered in detail all my questions about the *Havella*. And the questions were many. I was most interested in the ship that would take me into the remote waters of the world's sole remaining frontier.

She had a 150-horsepower diesel, 1,178 square feet of sail area, and was equipped with automatic steering, echo-sounder, direction finder, electric log, and radio telephone. Cruising easily at nine knots, she was a fifty-seven-foot, forty-ton copy of the famed Norwegian rescue boats, constructed with a double hull to protect her from the pack ice.

A few years before, I had traveled along the rocky coast of Norway, from Oslo to Bergen, with Captain Kristian Arntzen in the eighty-six-foot cruiser *Ambassador Bay*, and had learned a bit about rescue boats and their accomplishments off the Norwegian coast during World War II. Arntzen had been master of a rescue boat. The service was similar to our Coast Guard, but only slightly. It had no counterpart anywhere. It was volunteer winter work, with fifteen rescue ships, only a four- to six-man crew on each, braving gales and darkness to help boats in trouble.

That small fleet had saved 4,409 vessels from the sea and rescued 4,176 people, 266 of them from certain death along the treacherous coast. Captain Arntzen disgustedly told me of their toughest job, off Kristiansund in 1942, when the Germans were occupying Norway. They were called out in hurricane-force winds, a crew of four, to assist a ship that was breaking up on the rocks in the storm. It took most of the night and twelve trips in lifeboats to save forty Nazis, two Norwegians, and a dog.

The German port captain in Kristiansund wanted the names of the crew of the rescue squad so they could be awarded the Iron Cross. No Norwegian wanted such an "honor" so the captain of the rescue vessel said bluntly, "A daily job merits no reward."

The German captain was insulted. His country's highest honor, or one of them, was being refused, but he saved face by announcing publicly in Kristiansund that the Norwegians were heroes. That, recalled Captain Arntzen, was like being congratulated for having leprosy.

The aristocrats of their profession, Norwegian seamen can be blunt to the point of rudeness, but, if they accept you, I have found that they are among the best people on earth. And if you go down to the sea with them in their ships, you discover an entirely new dimension in life. I had been aboard several Norwegian vessels—a freighter sailing the Great Lakes from Montreal to Duluth, Minnesota, a fishing smack, and two others—enough to know that, if there is any such thing, then Norwegians are masters of the sea. So, although I realized that we would be traveling dangerous waters, I had few qualms. None about the Norwegians, but some about myself. I would be with superb seamen, on a ship that was staunchly built. What bothered me most was simply anxiety to meet the crew.

This was the last leg, the journey by diesel ketch to the land where no one had been, to the silent place created by the Chinese Wall Front Glacier. At this point, I didn't like to think of it as the last leg, but as the first part of a round trip. There is not much you can do about personal qualms; the mind takes over at times like these and dictates its own terms. Right now my brain was telling me that seeking adventure complicated my life. Why, my mind wondered, wasn't I content with getting away from the mundane by simpler means, such as kayaking down a remote river, or cross-country skiing alone in an isolated New England area, or back-packing into mountains in Montana, or even hiking along the Appalachian trail? No, not you, it grumbled, you have to do it the hard way, take two planes, a bus, an old steamship that almost shook you loose from the little sense you had left, and put you here in this forlorn place to search for another that is even more desolate.

In a small boat, with people you don't know, in the land that God forgot. Good planning.

So I just stood there on the shore letting spirit and common sense clash and watched the *Havella* for fully twenty minutes before approaching and introducing myself. The crew came on deck several times and I thought about those five men I would be with for some time. Bolin had said that they worked on the *Havella* because they liked the freedom it gave them. They were responsible to no one but themselves—and the sea.

What they were was obvious. They were Vikings. Direct descendants of the Norsemen who came out of the north in what were called "hordes," raiding most of the then known world, exploring it far beyond its recognized barriers, subduing an area slightly smaller than the Roman Empire. Indomitable, fierce men, they made such a strong impression from the eighth century to the middle of the eleventh that the period was called The Age of the Vikings.

Students of linguistics do not see eye to eye on the origin of the word "Viking." They agree that it is an old Norse term for a seagoing buccaneer, but explain that it could come from several sources. A possible source is *vikja,* or deviate, meaning that a Viking is one who leaves home to journey. The Norse word *vik,* creek or inlet, makes sense, inasmuch as the Norwegian Vikings lived along fjords. Also *vig,* battle, is favored, for all Vikings loved to fight. It was part of their religion. Vikings who died in battle were carried by Valkyries to heaven, Valhalla, where the fallen warriors lived forever, banqueting daily with the gods. On the other hand, many Norwegians believe that Viking came from *Viken,* which simply means men from the Vik region near Oslo.

I had been in that region and had seen, in "The Hall of the Viking Ships," the three ships first discovered in burial mounds in 1867. They were black, over seventy feet long, and one, the Gokstad ship, had sixteen pairs of oars and a sail. A replica constructed in 1893 proved how well the Vikings built their ships. It crossed the Atlantic in less than a month.

Historians believe that this type of ship was a mere pleasure craft, and that the Viking raiding vessels were more seaworthy, and were at least one hundred feet long, with room for twenty pairs of oarsmen. These were the dreaded long ships, the *dreki,* or dragon ships that made England, Scotland, and Ireland easy prizes, that sailed up Europe's Rhine and Seine rivers, attacked Paris, reached Spain, and were rowed through the Strait of Gibraltar into the Mediterranean. Their most courageous voyages took them to Iceland, Greenland, and the coast of North America.

It is impossible to stand on a far northern shore and watch Norwegians make a ship ready for cruising without thinking about their forebears, who virtually conquered the world with wooden ships, oars, and axes. The Viking's ax not only felled the trees to build his ships, but was a weapon that brought terror to all of Christendom.

What brought the sea-roving feats of the Vikings across to me most strongly was the sudden realization that these supermen had rowed, yes, rowed, huge wooden ships in water far wilder than that which the *Lyngen* had been through in bringing me here. It was incredible.

I realized also that, unlike their ancestors, the seamen on the *Havella* were reserved, that, unless I was many hours late, they would not search Longyearbyen for me. I could stand here dreaming about the old Vikings for another hour and not be disturbed. Unless pretty well relaxed with aquavit, Norwegians never thrust themselves upon you. They would be waiting for me on their ship. *Havella*'s gangway was my welcome mat. It was out.

I walked it and found the five seamen waiting for me, dressed in heavy-knit sweaters, a bold reminder that I was in the true north where summer was a matter of semantics.

I said hello and, almost as one man, the crew greeted me. As they came across the deck, it was like flipping the pages of Joseph Conrad. First, Haakon Godtliebsen, the captain, stumped toward me with a game leg, so real in his role that he seemed false, like a stock character in a sea drama. He was five ten, with beefy shoulders, icy blue eyes, yellow hair, a long jaw, and a soft voice.

Sigurd Dal was the ice pilot. His bold face could have been that of a Viking jarl, an earl of the fjords, carved from wood to fit onto the prow of a dragon ship. Big, blocky, full of authority, he took my hand in a firm grip and announced in guttural tones that he was honored to have me aboard.

The youngest crew member was Alf Olsen, the mate, with tousled blond hair and calm stone-gray eyes; he came across the deck in a slouching walk, looking like Steve McQueen. Harald Hansen, the engineer, was the oldest, in his late sixties, wearing glasses, bald, with sun-leathered skin and a reassuring smile that opened his secretive Norwegian face and dropped twenty years from it.

The last man to shake hands in this "by rank" protocol introduction was short and slender, with a cap of sleek black hair reminding me that Norwegians were not always blond, that some had inherited the coloring of the women the Vikings had brought back as prizes from France, Spain, and Ireland. He needed a shave, deep lines radiated from somber brown eyes, as if cut with a knife. He bobbed his head.

"Aage Rutwold, steward," he said quickly, taking my bags, carrying them forward, beckoning with his head.

I followed him below to a lounge amidship, furnished with a small sofa, two cut-down versions of club chairs, two tables, three lamps, all firmly bolted to the deck. This comfortable lounge was prepared for some uncomfortable times. There were two double cabins, not large, but more than adequate, making the cabin on the *Lyngen* seem like a broom closet. There was a small head with a tiny shower, a spotless, well-equipped galley, and forward the crew's quarters.

The diesel muttered into life as I started up the hatchway after unpacking, the engine sawing like a leopard as we moved smoothly away from the quay. In minutes we were out of the harbor, swooping around the barges humped with coal. After the wallow of the *Lyngen*, the *Havella* felt as secure under my feet as the *Queen Mary*. The mountains of Longyearbyen poked black pagoda heads out of cloud mist as we quickly pulled away from the land, committing ourselves to the Arctic Ocean. Ice floes blossomed out of the water ahead like crystal flowers, the sun, bright as ever after the rain, striking prismatic blues and pinks in them.

Haakon Godtliebsen handled the *Havella* as easily as if she were a bicycle, taking her in a series of S curves around the ice. Sigurd Dal, the ice pilot, ignored the whole thing, standing staring at Longyearbyen fading into mist behind us. It would take more complicated ice than we were now encountering to get Dal involved. I began to see exactly where I was—at the top of the world, where many before me had toppled off—a place where an ice pilot could be the most important person I would ever know.

Not far from Longyearbyen a spit of land slashed out into the sea like a sickle, its point narrow, broadening as it cut back inland.

The captain suddenly stuck his head out of the wheelhouse. "We go in. Show you some strange animals."

He took the *Havella* in an abrupt left turn, bringing her about and close into the arm of land.

Alf Olsen and Sigurd Dal winched the small boat on the port side down into the water. Olsen didn't bother with the small outboard. He rowed us, saying that when we got ashore we must be silent and walk as quietly as we could in order not to spook the animals. Like the captain, he didn't tell me what the animals were.

There was snow on the ridges farther back, but I could see no baleful glare of a glacier here. The land was rocky and vegetation sparse and brown. With Olsen leading, we traveled for about two miles, until he stopped, held up a hand, signaling me. I walked quietly to his side.

They stood, primitive animals come alive from the paintings of Cro-Magnon man on the cave walls of France's Les Eyzies. I didn't know what they were.

"Musk ox," Olsen whispered, his gray eyes gleaming.

As we walked closer, I could see their brown eyes through the shaggy hair that nearly covered their faces. They were carefully watching us. As we continued to advance, a big bull grumbled, did a graceful little two-step forward threatening us. He pranced six feet toward us. We stopped in our tracks.

Nosing the three calves into the center of a quickly formed semicircle, the adults closed into a complete circle, heads down, glaring at us. It was a tight, impregnable fortress of massive, horned flesh guarding the calves. The musk oxen's heads were moving from side to side as they faced us, clearly exposing the odd, yoke-shaped horns. Coming down either side, recurving into a hook with stiletto-sharp points, the twenty-five-inch horns nearly joined in the center of the head, forming a bony helmet about ten inches wide at the base. Both males and females had them, the males' heavier and longer.

The musk oxen were smaller than domestic bulls, their bodies blocky, legs and neck short, shoulders slightly humped, tails stubby. The twenty-inch-long hair covering their bodies was brownish-black, paling on the middle of the back and lower legs.

These were part of a herd of about fifty on Spitsbergen Island, the offspring of seventeen young released there in 1929. Norway also transplanted musk ox to the Dovre mountain plateau in central Norway in 1932. Earlier transplants to Gurskøy Island near Alesund on Norway's west coast didn't take. It was thought that the grass there was unsuitable, and some of the animals died when they toppled off steep precipices.

Scientists apparently were confused when they named the musk ox *Ovibos moschatus*, literally "sheep-cow." The hairy animal is not a sheep, a cow, or an ox. Its nearest surviving relative is the Takin, a goat-antelope from the highlands of central Asia. But the men who named the animals can be forgiven, for only in recent years have biologists working in Greenland, Canada, and Alaska begun to learn hard facts about the musk ox. Its habitat was so remote and forbidding that the only word or description of the mysterious musk ox was carried by hunters or explorers, some of it misleading, much hearsay.

Today we recognize two, the Barren Ground, *Ovibos moschatus moschatus*, on the North American mainland; and the northern subspecies of Greenland and Arctic islands, *Ovibos moschatus wardi*.

A true ancient, the musk ox's ancestors roamed the arctic prairies, steppes, and tundra of north-central Asia one million years ago. They were the contemporaries of the mammoth and the woolly rhinoceros, and also two giant musk oxen, *Bootherium* and *Symbos*. Of this prehistoric group only the musk ox as we now know it has survived. My feeling in Svalbard that I was watching ancient animal paintings from cave walls come alive was not far off, for the musk ox was thriving during the time of Neanderthal and Cro-Magnon artists.

The musk ox came to Europe and America during the Ice Age, when the great glaciers lowered oceans, permitting animals to travel across a land bridge joining Asia and Alaska. Moving with the glaciers, the musk ox traveled as far as Iowa. As the glaciers melted and retreated, musk oxen and other arctic-oriented animals managed to survive only in true northern regions of North America and Greenland. Changes of climate also made the animals extinct in Europe and Asia.

Musk oxen lived as long as they did because they favored that harsh habitat called the "high arctic," a world of extremes, where enemies and competition for food were minimized; and they were animals designed especially for survival in places where it seemed impossible. This was a world, bordering the tundras, edging polar seas, where winter ruled much of the time, where vegetation was sparse, wind high, temperatures below zero. Strangely, though, the so-called high arctic has little snow. It is, in effect, a far northern desert, with a yearly precipitation of as little as ten inches. Generally less than fifteen inches, snowfall there never exceeds thirty inches a year. Musk oxen can penetrate ice and snow for food with their sharp, horny hooves, but they prefer the exposed, wind-bared slopes where they can easily find what scrubby vegetation exists.

Musk oxen feed mainly on dwarf shrubs, sedges, and grass; crowberries and willows are favorite foods, along with beach rye grass, but these animals do not care much for lichen, the main staple of caribou, so the two do well on the same ranges. Social animals, musk oxen gather in herds of four to fifteen, sometimes three times that many. Polygamous, summertime herds are headed by a big bull, the harem consisting of cows, calves, and immature musk oxen. In warm weather, grown bulls without harems are loners, but in winter they are often seen as part of harems, or in their own bachelor groups.

Breeding time, late summer, with the bulls in angry rut, produces some mighty combats in contest for harems. The battles often continue until the loser is gored to death or staggers off to nurse his wounds in solitude. The result of this bloody business is one calf, twenty inches long, weighing about twenty pounds, born in April or early May, when the temperature may still be as low as thirty degrees below zero, and the matter of survival precarious, despite the thick brown, curly coat the calf is born with. It huddles under its mother until it is dry, then, precocious, within a few hours can keep up with its mother in the herd. Although it feeds on its mother's milk, rich in lactose, protein, and fat, for three months, it also begins to nibble on grass and plants within a couple of weeks, instinctively preparing for its complete weaning at four months. Musk oxen are not only protective mothers, but shower their offspring with care, attention, and affection.

Growth is rapid for the first year, the calf putting on as much as two hundred pounds. This rapidity cuts back though, and normal adult size is not attained until five or six years of age (average size for males, 750 pounds, females 540). Life span is about twenty years. Musk oxen are not prolific; females do not breed until the third year, never having more than a single calf, which often doesn't survive under the Arctic's own cruel system of birth control. They generally breed only every other year, rarely while nursing a calf. Thus observers have recorded many large herds without a single calf. Also, musk oxen seem to be able to work out their own system of birth control. In one Alaskan experiment, the number of calves fell from 25 to 10 percent of the population as the number of musk oxen reached the near limit of their food supply.

Polar bears, grizzlies, and wolves may take a few calves, but with the unique protective circle the musk oxen employ when threatened, even the skilled and strong tundra wolves do not persist. Stubborn wolves have been seen staying near the circle, with male musk oxen taking turns to break ranks briefly and attack them, then with military precision closing the circle again. There is one case of musk oxen being attacked by a large black bear. He managed to kill one, but the others gored him to death.

Musk oxen look clumsy, but as I saw in Spitsbergen with the bull that threatened us, they are agile and fast, and have been seen making right-angle turns at a gallop over rough country. Their hooves are constructed to spread on slippery terrain, with edges that are sharp enough to grip the ground. Their horns are among the sharpest and most effective of any animal, and their courage is great.

Eskimos gave the musk ox a colorful name, "Oomingmuk," the bearded one. It is apropos and more accurate than the scientific one, as the animal's muzzle is covered with hair, and long tufts droop from each side of the lower jaw. It was that hairy hide, which often reaches more than three feet in length, with a woolly underlayer, that nearly wiped out the musk ox. It protected him from the coldest temperatures, but once it was discovered that the undercoat, called "qiviut" by the Eskimos, was softer, warmer, and more valuable than cashmere, the animal was in trouble.

Musk oxen were once abundant in Alaska, on the coasts of eastern and northern Greenland, and in the Arctic islands of Canada. With the arrival of white men, traders and whalers, also came danger. Not only were Eskimos supplied with guns, with which they easily killed many more musk oxen than they normally would have, but the white men shot thousands for food and that prized undercoat, which was made into robes. The Hudson's Bay Company alone bought nearly twenty thousand. In one period explorers in the far north of Canada killed over a thousand musk oxen for food. Many young were captured alive for the world's zoos by a simple and effective method: All the fiercely protective adults were killed first.

By the middle of the nineteenth century, this rare animal that nature had protected for eons by equipping it to live in the brutal, barren Arctic, was down to less than a thousand in all of Canada. Those in Greenland were nearly gone, and the Alaskan musk oxen were completely wiped out. The last small herd there was killed by Eskimos a little over a century ago.

In 1930, E. W. Nelson, first Chief of the U. S. Bureau of Biological Survey, asked Congress to appropriate $40,000 for the purchase of musk oxen in Greenland. Convinced by Nelson that the animal was not only rare and had a potential domestic value, but that it was part of our wildlife heritage, Congress complied—and the musk ox, luckier than the buffalo, was saved.

Thirty-four of the Greenland calves and yearlings were quartered at the University of Alaska in 1931, and carefully studied. In 1935 and 1936, the thirty-one animals that remained were transferred to Alaska's Nunivak Island, which had been reserved for them as a National Wildlife Refuge. By 1968 that experimental seed herd had increased to seven hundred and fifty.

As they overgrew the range, musk oxen were successfully transplanted to their original ranges. They have increased their numbers to about fifteen hundred; Canada has nearly ten thousand. They are now completely protected everywhere.

A naturalist once said that it is the tendency of the polar regions to be rich in individuals and poor in species. Anything that lives in the far north, musk ox or man, must survive through strength of character. I would see more interesting survivors.

We talked about the musk oxen all the way back to the *Havella*, and on board for another hour. Suddenly Sigurd Dal tapped my shoulder. He showed me a small white whale breaking the surface on the port side, rolling like a log, more blue than white, its blowing breath a spray of iridescence above the water. The crew pointed and chattered in Norwegian like boys, excited about a sight that they must have seen many times. This gave me instant assurance that I was in the hands of responsive, enthusiastic men who loved what they were doing above all else. And, as sometimes happens, that first impression was firmly correct.

Now well away from land, the crew busied themselves at their individual jobs, Hansen below with his engine, Olsen coiling a rope, Dal testing the lifeboat pulleys, Aage Rutwold below making kitchen sounds, the captain at the wheel.

I looked back. The whale was still lolling on the surface, reminding me that whales had brought men and trouble to Svalbard. Barents reported that these waters teemed with whales. Soon the Arctic Ocean was aswarm with whaling ships, the hunters, Dutch, English, Basque, French, Hanseatic, Danish, Norwegian.

Competition for the whales was so fierce that naval escorts had to sail with the whalers to protect them. Whales were so valuable that a single giant might pay for an entire expedition. This wealth in the sea led to international complications, until in 1618 the British and the Dutch decided to divide the coast between them, with the 79th parallel the dividing line. Fortified stations were established on some of the islands. But greed was the final arbitrator, and the fight for the whales and walruses ended only when most of them were wiped out. In 1605, one hunter, Steven Bennett, of the Muscovy Company, killed enough walruses to produce eleven tons of oil. Between 1669 and 1778 the Dutch alone took 57,500 whales.

I asked Olsen what the whale and walrus situation was right now. He put down his rope, looked back at the white whale, and said, "We see them again. A few. They are mostly protected."

He joined me at the rail and we stood watching the *Havella* cut through flat ice floes it couldn't avoid, the severed pieces floating behind us like great slices of angel food cake. I asked him about his work and how long he had been aboard the *Havella*, finding that the reserve I had encountered in Tromsø, and expected here, was much less than anticipated. He laughed, pointed at his blond head, and said, "I got coal dust in there. I've been away from the mines and on the *Havella* three years, but I still smell the coal that I cut with a saw, and I wake up at three o'clock in the morning and smell the lime in the pits and hear the explosions going off in galleries all around and I think every dark place I enter is the mountain. But the captain tells me another few months I'll forget I ever dug coal."

Not yet thirty, he had also sailed on seal-hunting vessels for ten years. He would talk about it, but only generally, telling me that the harp seals were the most valuable, and that fur of the newborn and seal blubber were what hunters were after.

There were three main breeding grounds for the seals, in the drift ice off northern Newfoundland and southeastern Labrador, at the mouth of the White Sea on the Arctic coast of Europe, and the area where Olsen hunted, "The Western Ice," between Iceland and Svalbard. "It's best there in the Norwegian Sea north of Jan Mayen Island," he said. "But it's hard, cold work. Last of March is when the season opens."

He didn't mention the actual killing of the seals, just saying that the pelt of the baby harp is white and very soft, the rich fur known as "whitecoat," and that they were caught when the females crawled up on ice floes to whelp their young. The round trip to the sealing grounds took six weeks, but the ships carried provisions for three months in case they were caught in the ice.

The crew of Olsen's ships usually consisted of sixteen, eleven doing the actual seal hunting. He said that the last time out his ship had taken a thousand seals, harp and hooded, worth about $17,000. The crew worked on the share system.

"For six weeks' work," he said, grinning without humor, "I brought home two hundred and ninety dollars."

There was a long silence. We could hear the captain humming at the wheel. He sounded happy.

"The Captain also was a sealer," Olsen finally said. "Longer than me. Also a mate when he was in his twenties, like me. I hope some day to have my own ship too."

There it was, the dream of nearly every male Norwegian who lived by the sea. Master a ship, master the sea.

It was about forty degrees, and I wondered aloud what kept it that warm here in a land buried in glaciers.

"Even right now in late July," Olsen said, "it could drop below freezing. But it probably won't."

He explained that the warm Gulf Stream, running along the west and north coasts, makes it possible to sail farther north in ice-free water—as far as 82° N latitude—than anyplace else on the globe.

"But there's also another current," he said, "a cold stream that sweeps from the sea to the east of Svalbard, moving around South Cape, continuing north along the west coast of Norway between the land and the Gulf Stream. As we get closer to shore that cold current always reminds us where we are."

Surprising me, he began talking about the Gulf Stream, adding that most seamen either drank and read, or drank and drank, or maybe just read, to pass the time. He read. One book that he had read was Matthew Maury's *The Physical Geography of the Sea*.

" 'There is a river in the ocean,' " he quoted. " 'In the severest drought it never fails, and in the mightiest floods it never overflows. Its banks and its bottoms are of cold water, while its current is of warm. The Gulf of Mexico is its fountain, and its mouth is in the Arctic Seas. It is the Gulf Stream. There is in the world no other such majestic flow of waters. Its current is more rapid than the Mississippi or the Amazon, and its volume more than a thousand times greater.' "

I probably shouldn't have been surprised to have the mate aboard a ketch in the Arctic Ocean give me facts about the Gulf Stream that I never knew. Olsen was only researching and reading about the element that controlled his life. The sea.

Somewhat abashed, he confirmed this with what came out like an apology. "We on ships up here are all interested in the Gulf Stream. It makes our world go."

All the crew spoke English with a heavy accent. Olsen's English was the best, but you had to pay attention when any of them talked. We discussed language and Olsen gave me some keys to why some words in English came out the way they did. He was bright, still in a learning age where he picked up everything, and he listened carefully when I talked, which made me watch my language. It made me realize what I suppose I had known all along, but hadn't had accented before. The American language is rapidly pulling away from the English, studding itself with slang, colloquialisms, half words, regional expressions, televisionese, bureaucratic double-talk, sloppy thought and phrasing. Before I had been on the *Havella* a day I decided to chop "okay," "right," "you know," and "would you believe" from my vocabulary.

Olsen told me that the Scandinavian languages shared many characteristics. The letter "w" is pronounced like a "v" in English, the "j" like "y." "Ø" in Norwegian is pronounced like the "u" in "burn." "Sj" and "skj" are "sh" and the double "aa" is pronounced like the "o" in "gourd," the "ae" is like the "a" in "rat." The captain's first name, "Haakon," came out "Hawkun." Looking at "Arøsund" on the chart with Olsen, I found that he made it "Awrasun."

It never became a problem. I might miss a couple of words in each sentence that was directed at me, but it was a far cry from falling back upon a sort of sign language, as I had in the central jungles of India, and more rewarding than many of my struggles with French menus.

Naturally the crew communicated with one another in their own tongue. That very first day I mentioned to Alf Olsen that at times the language had an almost oriental lilt to it.

He laughed. "You mean Chinese? It makes about as much sense." Then he told me about Norway's two languages.

In 1914 when Denmark officially surrendered possession of Norway to Sweden, Norway's language was supposed to be Riksmål, a Danish dialect spoken mainly by the upper class. The several dialects used by the rest of the people came from old Norse, the language of the thirteenth-century sagas, and had no written form.

Nationalists urged that Riksmål be given strength by having more Norwegian words added to it. While this was being attempted, a rural linguist invented Landsmål, consisting of the several dialects in use, but giving them a written form. Patriotism made it an immediate success and its popularity pushed it into first rank as the official language. While Landsmål and Riksmål are both taught in the schools, there are still frequent hot-tempered squabbles over which one should be the national language. So most Norwegians can speak both.

At that point Aage Rutwold came up from his galley and said something loudly in Norwegian Chinese. The sound had the same ring in any language. Dinner.

"Cod," said Olsen, and my heart sank. Did Norwegians know nothing but fish? They had probably taken on some cod from the trawler back at Longyearbyen, from those boats that had smelled so overwhelmingly of the fish that I had preferred the smell of coal dust.

Rutwold looked smart in crisp white. And he didn't smell fishy. Hopefully, I followed the crew below.

We ate amidships (except Olsen, who was at the wheel), the table set with a starched white cloth, Danish stainless, and sturdy goblets. Rutwold brought warm plates, observing sea protocol by serving the captain first. I had never eaten cod cooked this way. It had been poached. Tender, flaky white pieces were drenched with melted sweet butter; tart mustard sauce was passed, along with tiny new boiled potatoes rolled in butter and chopped fresh parsley.

Øl, beer, *Bokkøl*, dark beer, full-bodied, full of flavor, was poured. Everything was going to be all right.

We talked about cod for a while. I had eaten it before, as has just about everyone. But I knew little about the fish. Every man on the *Havella* had at one time or another served time on a cod trawler. As far as Norwegians were concerned cod was the beef of the sea. Codfishing was a national industry.

I had one question. What makes this large fish taste so delicate?

"Delicate?" said the captain. "Being very fresh, and the way Aage cooked it helps. But the big cod itself feeds on clams, mussels, crabs, and small fish. It fills its flesh with the best flavor of the sea almost as soon as it opens its mouth."

They talked about the fish while we drank Aage Rutwold's strong, fresh-perked coffee. Cod range both sides of the Atlantic, from the northern Barents Sea, where our fish was caught, to the Bay of Biscay and near Greenland and Iceland. In the spring, when fishing is best, it is not unusual for a trawler to net thirty-five tons on a single trip. They are considered ground fish, but Hansen, the engineer, had been on trawlers where they had been caught in waters of all depths, from one fathom to two hundred. He remembered one that was six and a half feet long and weighed over two hundred pounds, but most caught for market are from twenty-five to forty inches long and range in weight from ten to twenty pounds.

In the North Atlantic alone seven billion pounds of cod are caught every year. The captain worried aloud about overfishing, and said that Norway had been studying that problem since 1860, had even thought of artificial propagation, but gave it up and instead concentrated on research, studying the age and growth of cod in Norwegian waters. How did this help? It gave fishery experts the age at which cod should be caught, allowing others to mature and spawn at least once before they were netted. A single female spawned from three to nine million eggs. But the eggs are preyed upon by many marine creatures and only a small percentage become adult fish.

There were reports of very poor spawning in the Barents Sea. The captain was concerned and thought that the problem was caused by the mysterious disappearance of capelin, a small fish that the cod preferred. Hansen said that there ought to be new regulations on the size of nets, the mesh should be wider to allow more young fish to escape.

Cod? Ask a Norwegian seaman a question about that fish

and you've got a nonstop conversation. This one was broken up by the captain going to relieve Olsen at the wheel.

Back on deck, the constant hard golden sun smote the ice cap to the north, flaring it a vivid blue, the light splintering back on the water before us. That was the central Svalbard ice cap on a high plateau, its sides deeply trenched by radial valleys, most of which contained glaciers. We would advance on Gresswell's Ice Age nautical mile by nautical mile and follow its coastline to our destination.

Meanwhile, after more than four hours out of Longyearbyen, we had about ten hours to first landfall.

"We will stop at Ny Alesund," Olsen said. "King's Bay. Small coal mine there. Maybe fifty people. Most northerly settlement in the world. And the last we'll see. But I'm thinking you'll be glad to leave it."

He went on to say that the remains of the hangar where Amundsen kept his airship are still there.

Olsen didn't say what airship, and, of course, everyone had to know who Amundsen was.

7

"Look!" Captain Godtliebsen said, spinning the *Havella* into the dock. "Coming now across the *bukt* is a seal. See how he comes!"

Even from a distance the seal was black and shiny, the sun highlighting him. He was swimming straight for us from the far side of the bay.

We were still in motion and it seemed odd that the animal would be making directly for us. Weren't seals shy, especially here in sealing country?

Although there had been plenty of floe ice we hadn't seen a single seal until now. About fifteen hours after we left Longyearbyen we had swung from the open sea closer to shore along Prins Karls Forland, the island all sharp peaks and angles, forbidding as a volcano. As I stood beside the captain at the wheel he told me how tricky navigation was here, explaining that usually the inshore waters were not safe, but these were. It was the middle of the sound that was too shallow, except for small boats. He pointed out the northern point, Forlandet—"Fuglehuken," he called it—and its automatic revolving light, warning of the danger in the sound. Even in sunlight its blinking eye could be seen, the only sign that man had ever been this way. Farther north there was a spit of land, misty in the distance. Cape Mitra.

"Ny Alesund. King's Bay ahead," the captain said, as we finally came up a stretch of calm fjord water, Kongsfjord, passing or sometimes going through flat floes that parted with the sound of breaking glass.

He said that King's Bay was ideally situated, not hemmed in by mountains as were most of the other islands. "This is the reason," he said, "why the polar explorers trying to get to the North Pole by air used King's Bay as their base camp."

The two large glaciers glaring in the sun beyond were Kongsvegen and Kongsbreen. The captain apparently knew the name of every glacier that was visible and spoke of them as if they were living characters. For the first time I could feel their very real menace.

In the harbor, as the *Havella* approached, were two weather-beaten fishing trawlers and several smaller boats. The few houses and buildings beyond looked like an unused Hollywood mining town set. Except for spirals of smoke drifting from some chimneys, it seemed abandoned.

We bumped gently against the dock. That was when the captain saw the seal.

It veered around the trawlers and kept a straight line for us, just its black head above water. As we watched, the weird goggle eyes grew, became enormous. Hind feet came splashing out of the water. But seals have no hind feet.

Treading water now, the seal said, "Hi! Any Americans aboard?"

The captain and his mate were speechless. I, knowing that the captain was a seal expert, was dumfounded.

What was a man, obviously an American, doing playing seal in an Arctic bay, so far north that it isn't on most maps, swimming in water so cold that it could freeze a human being in minutes?

He came closer in easy overhand strokes, and Alf and I reached over and helped him aboard. He came up tall, dripping water from a frogman's black rubber suit. Taking off his goggles and helmet, he introduced himself. Fred Baldwin from New York City. After introductions, the captain still staring at Baldwin, the blond, blue-eyed young man explained what he was doing here.

The explanation was as astonishing as his appearance in King's Bay Harbor.

He was staying here in a Nissen hut with a Swedish photographer who was recording life in the north, and this was as far as they could get. He, Baldwin, had another target, polar bears.

"What do you want with *isbjørn?*" The captain finally broke his shocked, half-embarrassed silence brought on by his identifying Baldwin in the harbor as a seal. He used the Norwegian name, ice bear, for the polar bear.

"I've got assignments from two national magazines for photo spreads," Baldwin said. "*If* I can pull it off. I want to photograph polar bears underwater. *Me,* I'll be under the water. Photographing them on top, swimming, killing seals. Anything I can get."

The captain stared at him in obvious disgust. "*Isbjørn* lives on seals. The seals are black and shiny in the water. Like you in that rubber suit. You will be eaten alive!"

"He is right, Mr. Baldwin," Alf Olsen said quietly. "We thought you were a seal in the bay. And me, I've seen more seals in my life than people."

Baldwin avoided their flat warnings by changing the subject. "I was practicing in the bay. Getting my wind. This suit is beautifully insulated. Didn't feel the cold at all. I can do that bay in nothing flat. Next time I'll swim underwater with the cameras. Do the thing in stages until I know what I'm up against."

His logic didn't deter the Norwegians. The captain wondered if he would take a man with a gun along. Baldwin shook his head, and the captain reminded him that it is a matter of record that polar bears attack men, that just about anything that moves in the north the bears consider game. Food.

"About every explorer who lived to write about it recorded polar bear attacks," Alf Olsen said.

Baldwin spent another ten minutes trying to convince us that he really wasn't crazy, explaining that professional photography had become so competitive, with so many expert and imaginative practitioners, that he had finally decided that his sure way to success was specialization. Liking the out-of-doors, he had decided to concentrate on the unusual in nature.

"Got some good stuff in Lapland on reindeer herds. Went right into a herd and did some reindeer-eye views. A few months ago I went underwater and photographed a marlin being hooked. Bit sticky at times with that big fish thrashing around down there. But it turned out."

The captain shook his head, giving up on Baldwin, and clumped below to help Rutwold check the stores. Alf Olsen and I went with Baldwin to meet the Swedish photographer and spent a half hour with them drinking Norwegian beer, talking about their plans.

Their Nissen hut had a little coal-burning stove with a coffeepot sitting on its lid, a small linoleum-covered table, two straight-backed wooden chairs, and a lamp on the table. That was it. Sleeping bags were spread on the floor. Their camera equipment was in sturdy strapped leather cases in a far corner.

They didn't think they'd be able to get any farther north than King's Bay. But this was well up in Svalbard and they were hopeful that there would be bears around. Olsen told them there probably would be, the bears were all over Svalbard, and in the summer spent much time in the water.

I talked in generalities about why I was here, saying that I also was interested in polar bears, but studying them from a greater distance than Baldwin planned.

He laughed and said, "Chicken!" and asked me if I'd call his agent in New York when I got back. She hadn't heard from him in months and he figured that with my transportation I'd get away from Svalbard sooner than he would.

Olsen and I then walked around King's Bay. It was drab, gray, the dozen or so houses shabby, unpainted, one with two small children and several ducks playing in the weedy yard beside it; another had a small greenhouse with lettuce, carrots, rhubarb, and bright pansies that looked as incongruous as orchids in this place.

The mines that stood silent, cable cars rusting, tall, skeletal coal conveyors, dominated King's Bay. Olsen, without going into detail about the experience, said that he had worked here for a short period and explained that the King's Bay Coal Company had started in 1916 and continued until the late thirties. Mining was begun again at the beginning of World War II, when Norway was short of coal. But the miners finally had to be evacuated to England in 1941.

"The mines opened again in 1945," Olsen said. "Then in 1953 a mine disaster stopped all work. Several times they tried to start again but accidents and just plain bad luck has mostly kept them out of business. They mine some coal still, but not much."

He showed me the old square building that used to be the North Pole Hotel before World War II, then was taken over by the mine officials. We looked at the small power station, the beating heart of the settlement, and walked through an old graveyard, the weathered, chipped granite tombstones all with

Dutch names and the year 1600, whale hunters and trappers, Olsen said.

There was a sad aura about the place, it was a ghost town, peopled by past events and shattered dreams. Baldwin and the Swedish photographer would pump life into it for a while, and so would the few ships and fishing trawlers that pulled in occasionally. But that was it.

Because of its location, Olsen thought that King's Bay might have a future with meteorologists and scientists. He had heard that it could become a satellite tracking station and also that the Norwegian Polar Institute might establish a station here.

Put Longyearbyen and King's Bay together and you had most of the Norwegians and the buildings that Svalbard had to offer. How many people? Maybe a thousand at Longyearbyen and fifty at King's Bay. Buildings? One hundred would be stretching it. How many Russians in their mines at Barentsburg near Longyearbyen? Fifteen hundred? There were several meteorological and radio stations on the islands manned by small crews, and sometimes a few trappers and fishermen came to Svalbard. Other than that, in an area larger than Belgium or West Virginia, this was a land without people. In a world where even Alaska is becoming overcrowded, and Eskimos hunt from snowmobiles (those few who still hunt) and live in housing developments, Svalbard may be the last place on earth where man can catch his breath without taking in carbon monoxide.

But Olsen had been right when he said I'd be happy to leave King's Bay. I hadn't come to Svalbard to look at its sad man-made scenery. Olsen had something else he wanted to show me, after he checked back with the *Havella* to see if he was needed. As we walked to the harbor, the *Brandal*, a two-masted, coal-burning trawler belching black smoke came grunting in.

In less than ten minutes seamen were pouring off. Two approached me as I stood looking at the old fishing craft. They were small men with leathered skin and eyes bright as blue topaz. Their clothing was wrinkled and smelled strongly of fish. Black rubber boots came to their knees, their hands were red, chapped, and there was a beaten air about them. I couldn't understand what they were saying, and wished that I could. The hardness of the sea was in their faces, cut in sharp lines around the mouth and eyes; one held his soiled knitted cap in his hand while he tried to talk to me.

Olsen came out on the *Havella*'s deck and spoke to the men in Norwegian. They waved cheerily at him and walked on toward the cluster of buildings in King's Bay.

"Codfishermen," Olsen said soberly. "They lead a tough life, hauling in trawl nets, cleaning fish, working in all kinds of weather, months on rough seas—" They had wanted to sell me a polar bear skin, Olsen said, to pick up some extra money to buy some whiskey in King's Bay. "If they didn't have a little cheer out of a bottle, they'd go daft."

He grinned and held up a brown paper bag, opening it, showing me two bottles of scotch. "Captain's orders to board the *Brandal* and make a trade. This for fresh halibut. If I have any luck you're in for a treat. Halibut out of these waters is the world's best."

He was back in minutes. "Business done. I'll be right with you. I want to show you where Amundsen kept his airship."

As I had learned almost immediately in Tromsø from Bolin's conversation about Amundsen and Nansen, Norwegians not only like to talk about their country's heroes, the explorers, but they are veritable fact books on them. Scratch a Norwegian and he begins spouting dates and places and accomplishments. Although it is all past history they do not consider it such, talking about them as if everything happened yesterday. As Americans know their sports figures, batting averages, games won, so do Norwegians know what happened in the history of their north country.

Alf Olsen was no exception. He walked me back beyond the settlement to higher ground and pointed out a mooring mast, and pieces of scrap iron and wood that looked like bleached bones.

"Signs of the life and death of Roald Amundsen," Olsen said. "He had the *Norge* here. But he also put King's Bay in world headlines in 1925 when he and your countryman Lincoln Ellsworth took off from here in two airplanes, the N-24 and N-25. It was the first attempt to reach the North Pole by air."

Amundsen, Ellsworth, and four others left King's Bay on May 21, 1925, in two Dornier flying boats. While taking off from the fjord where we came in on the *Havella*, one plane was damaged by ice. But they continued the flight and finally landed in open water at 88° N, about 125 miles from the Pole, where they had to leave one plane. For nearly a month the six men struggled to save the remaining plane from being crushed by pack ice, and finally succeeded by dragging it up on a floe.

They tried eight times to take off. Finally, dragging icy hummocks out of the way, tramping down the wet snow, they prepared a fifteen-hundred-foot runway, and just barely made it into the air. But before they reached King's Bay a faulty rudder forced them to make an emergency landing in the ice-cluttered sea off Svalbard's Northeast Land.

Standing by the rusted mooring mast that had launched both the *Norge* and General Umberto Nobile's *Italia*, Olsen told me about the feud between the two men, and the ironic story of Amundsen's death on what turned out to be a needless rescue mission. With the sea surrounding us, the glaciers hulking beyond, the gulls crying hoarsely over the harbor, it seemed as if it had happened that week.

When Amundsen and Ellsworth finally got back to King's Bay, they decided that an airship, a dirigible, might be more effective. Not concerned with speed and altitude, their still undeterred mission was to cross the polar cap of two and a half million square kilometers and chart that icy wasteland that had been explored only on its outer edges.

In a few months they found the airship, an Italian semi-dirigible, "N 1," designed by Umberto Nobile. Amundsen named it *Norge*, Norway, and planned an immediate expedition. He and Ellsworth would lead it, Nobile would be master of the airship.

In early May 1926 they flew it to King's Bay and found Admiral Richard Byrd and his Fokker plane, *Josephine Ford*, already there preparing for his North Pole flight. Umberto Nobile was disturbed and kept urging Amundsen and Ellsworth to take off immediately and reach the Pole first. Amundsen calmly told the Italian that they were not involved in any race, they were going to launch a scientific mission, and in any case Peary had already reached the Pole first. Byrd made the flight.

On May 11 Amundsen was ready and the *Norge* swung from the mooring mast ready to be launched. Seventy-two hours later the airship drifted over the North Pole. That flight over the Pole and across the unexplored basin of the Arctic to Cape Barrow and the landing at Teller on the Bering Sea dwarfed the Byrd accomplishment.

It also was the achievement of a lifetime goal for Amundsen. As the *Norge* passed over the Pole, the Norwegian, American, and Italian flags were dropped, which meant that Amundsen was the only man to plant his country's flag on both poles.

In the aftermath Nobile became irritated at the praise Amundsen received and announced to the world press that the credit for the *Norge*'s flight was due not to those who stood in the gondola watching the sights, but to the master of the ship who had skillfully guided it to its destination and brought it safely back. The Italian press claimed that the achievements of their country were not being acknowledged because of political differences. General Nobile summed up his rancor with, "The real polar explorer is the pilot."

For a while Amundsen ignored Nobile, but as the Italian continued the attack, the Norwegian suddenly counterattacked, revealing that Nobile had nearly wrecked the mission and the airship with his clumsy handling of it. He said that Nobile had also made serious errors in navigation, knew nothing of polar conditions, and, in fact, did not even know how to ski. He shrugged the Italian off as a military show-off and braggart.

Nobile raged for weeks, but finally the feud finished with much bitterness and resentment, only after Nobile had decided that he had found the answer to Amundsen's accusations.

He would show the Norwegian up in action, not words, by reaching the Pole in his own airship, the *Italia*, with an all-Italian crew.

Nobile flew his *Italia* to King's Bay and launched the airship on May 23, 1928. Early the next day he reached the Pole and cruised over it for two hours, sending out victorious messages to the world.

On the return trip suddenly all contact with the *Italia* was severed. The last message sent from the airship fixed its position at 120 miles from King's Bay.

Hemmed in by fog, the *Italia*, Nobile at the controls, had jammed her elevators, lost her trim, and smashed into drift ice, Nobile breaking his right arm and leg.

They had crashed on May 25, but finally by June 8 they were able to get messages out by wireless, giving their approximate location.

When he heard of the crash, Amundsen immediately volunteered to organize a rescue attempt. He announced that it could be done only by hydroplane or ice breaker, and cabled Ellsworth in America for assistance in finding a plane, but never received a reply.

The pleas for help kept coming from the Nobile expedition, the general himself saying, "You can depend upon Amundsen.

He is the real expert. He can organize a rescue party with sledges."

Russia's *Leonid Krassin*, then the world's largest and most powerful ice breaker, responded to the pleas for help and started from the Baltic Sea.

The French government sent its hydroplane *Latham*, which had been undergoing trials before trying for the world's long-distance straight-line flight record, from France to Jubuti, then across the Atlantic. Its pilot, René Guilibaud, and a crew of four were to fly to Tromsø and pick up Amundsen, the Arctic expert.

The *Latham* flew from Tromsø at four P.M. on June 18, 1928. Three hours later its radio signals were received, placing the plane about fifty nautical miles south of Bear Island. Nothing further was ever heard. Two months later a balance pontoon which had been secured to the *Latham*'s lower flywing was picked up in the ocean north of Tromsø.

Olsen angrily swung the rusty mooring mast. It creaked. He kicked a piece of gray wood from what had once been the *Norge*'s hangar. "Nine days after Amundsen disappeared, Lundborg, a Swedish pilot, took Nobile safely off the drift ice in a small ski-plane—"

Nobile's flight on the *Italia* to prove that he could reach the Pole in his own airship without the help of Norwegians also killed all but seven of the seventeen men who went along.

"Bankers, merchants, and shipowners sitting back in their offices in Oslo, Bergen, and Tromsø think men like those who wanted to go to the Pole were crazy," Olsen said bitterly. "Risking their lives, for what? Fame? They don't understand, and I can't speak your language good enough to tell you my feelings on it. A worm in your gut that makes you an individual? Pulls you out of the pack? I don't know. I don't have the education to know."

He said this just before we turned around and started back to the *Havella*, standing for a moment to take one last look at the high ground from which Amundsen made his leaps toward the Pole. As we walked along the quay to the harbor Olsen's eyes brightened when he saw the *Havella*.

"Floats there like a gull," he said softly. "When I ride her I feel like I'm flying." His calm gray eyes swung back to me. "Right now I'm glad to be flying away from this place. Too many memories."

As we approached the *Havella*'s gangway, he said, "You must be one of the crazy ones too, hey? Amundsen, Nansen, Byrd, Nobile, they wanted to get to the North Pole. You want to go to a lake and land lost from people for many years. Why? Can you tell me why?"

I considered it, the thoughts churning in my head. "No," I said, wanting to tell him maybe it was my own North Pole.

8

Hearing us on the gangway, the captain came on deck, looking sour.

"The engine is making some damn noises Hansen don't like. He won't let me take her out."

When I realized how much security the *Havella* had for me in this wild country, my stomach felt as if it had slipped to my knees. What would happen if Hansen couldn't fix it? Would we be stuck in King's Bay? Have to take one of the beat-up fishing trawlers out? Why would Hansen be upset about the engine so soon? Hadn't the ketch had a thorough check before we started? This didn't seem efficient, and I had thought that Norwegian seamen were perfectionists.

My face must have mirrored my thoughts.

The captain laughed, a barking, infectious sound. "Hansen's a grandmother to that engine of his. We'll lunch while he tinkers. It makes him happy."

This incident had an effect opposite to what I first experienced. Olsen went down and talked with Hansen before lunch and came back up smiling. "The engine just sounded a little rough. Harald likes his engines to always run smooth. Forty years as an engineer makes him a little hard to get along with."

So now I knew. Hansen was a perfectionist.

So was Aage Rutwold. His King's Bay lunch set a standard that never varied. Back in Tromsø Bolin had understated when he said the ketch had a good cook. The *Havella* had a chef.

First we had a very hot rich yellow noodle soup. The halibut Olsen bartered for on the *Brandal* came crusty-brown on top, so moist and white and delicate inside that it put down the finest chicken breast. Tiny carrots, looking suspiciously like those I had seen in the greenhouse when we toured King's Bay, and the little potatoes were served together in butter. Firm, sweet peaches, tasting home-canned, followed. It sounds plebian, but halibut so fresh that it almost hops is epicurean.

Havella quickly proved to be a cozy ship, with every man doing his job ably. Sigurd Dal, the ice pilot, hadn't had to exercise his expertise yet and I was hoping that perhaps in summer he might just be along for the ride, a member of a crew that remains an intact unit. That proved to be wishful thinking. But Dal didn't loaf, he took his turn at the wheel, and sat with the captain charting the course.

He was always at the bow when we cleared a harbor or encountered rough seas, and he had a seasoned air about him that gave a sense of security. The captain had told me that he had been an ice pilot for over twenty years and was one of the north's best. I believed it. Dal had that air about him, strongly reminiscent of that of the famed explorers, whether you know much about them or not. It was an indefinable aura that a few have, perhaps of authenticity and authority. It has been said that that was the appeal of Spencer Tracy, his authority as an actor, his ability to make you believe. Dal had that.

Harald Hansen was quiet, introspective. Besides loving

flowers (Olsen told me that he had an impressive garden in Tromsø and filled the windows and the tables in his house with flowerpots and potted plants that kept his wife busy when Hansen was at sea) he was fond of music and books. He could play a musical saw, and would later, but it took a lot of coaxing from the crew and he wouldn't do it until we had almost reached our destination. Often, when he wasn't with his engine, he could be found below, amidships, reading.

He found English difficult, a complicated language, but he would always try it and was careful with his words. I had no trouble understanding him, and liked to listen to him talk of Norway's literary giants, as he would whenever I steered the conversation that way. He didn't think much of most American writers, believing they are too preoccupied with sex and violence without valid reasons. And Henrik Ibsen was the world's greatest playwright. Hansen could be right about the man who wrote *Peer Gynt*, *A Doll's House*, *Hedda Gabler*, among others. Ibsen didn't write any of his great works until he was over fifty. Hansen didn't believe anyone under that age had fully developed their mental powers.

"Ibsen," Hansen said in his heavy accent, "was old enough to know what was wrong with the world. His comments and observations on the struggle between society and the individual have never been done better." The day he said that to me he took his glasses off and waved them violently. Without glasses his eyes looked very old, the color of faded denim. "Look what George Bernard Shaw said of Ibsen on our writer's seventieth birthday. 'His impact on England was almost equal to the influence which three revolutions, six crusades, a couple of foreign invasions and an earthquake would produce.'"

There were not any time-wasting chatter sessions. These were men dedicated to what they were doing, and they did not idly engage in conversation. Olsen was the exception, because I had talked at length to him first and usually went to him when there was something that puzzled me, or if there was information that I needed. But I never made the mistake of asking anything that wasn't pertinent. Of course there was little that wasn't. This was a strange, isolated world that few men ever see; the crew realized that and were proud of the land and the sea around it, and of the fact that they knew it as well as anyone alive.

As I like to cook, I had a built-in rapport with Aage Rutwold, but he was shy, soft-spoken, and rarely engaged anyone in conversation. If asked he would talk about his profession, and sometimes discuss food or what our menu would be a couple of days ahead. Olsen told me that he had worked in hotels and restaurants and could make more money ashore, but that he signed on the *Havella* because he liked the sea and the quiet of this northern world. "The silence," Olsen said soberly, "Aage likes the silence."

Three hours after we left King's Bay, Dal went to the bow and stood like one of his ancestors on a longboat, peering ahead. Even with the permanent sun there was mist and skeins of fog that drifted then came together woven into a blanket that would obscure vision immediately ahead for short periods. The *Havella* was making its nine knots, the hard surface of the sea thumping the bow. I hung onto a guardrail, watching waves like a wagging tail behind us. I wondered why the captain was going so fast, and why the ice pilot was at the bow. Usually when we were in a good sail across the sea everyone was relaxed but the man at the wheel.

Suddenly, as one patch of fog lifted, Sigurd Dal began muttering, then he shouted back to the captain.

Immediately Godtliebsen cut his speed and if a boat can go on cat feet that's what we were doing. Soon I saw why. "Nothing to get alarmed about," Dal said calmly. "There has been a change of wind to the northwest, which drove some ice from the ocean to this water closer to the coast." That frozen sea that the ancient adventurers had spoken of was sending some of its ice our way.

It looked like a mad sculptor had been at work. It wasn't pack ice and there wasn't a floating field of it as I had feared, but there were pieces of ice in any shape the imagination could conjure, a big hunk like a donkey, a giraffe, a perfect crystal orchid, a lion with sparkling mane, a filigreed sheet looking exactly like an oriental carpet. All of the ice objects floated on their backs and were mostly submerged, shining beneath the surface as green as polished jade.

On one side of us was the world's coldest, most dangerous ocean, on the other was the Svalbard archipelago, mountains that erupted out of the sea in frozen explosions of ice and rock. We could not travel too close to the islands because the waters were treacherous nearer that shallow, rock-lined shoreline, sometimes full of big ice where a glacier had just dropped a lusty calf. I had not yet seen a glacier up close; they hung there in the distance like huge cloud formations that never went away, with the constant foreboding aspect of a great storm in the making.

For two hours the *Havella* crunched cautiously through the ice, then we were suddenly free in water of a deep gray, the pewter color produced by melting ice. As the sun polished the sea to aluminum, I discovered something I must have known but never thought about.

None of the crew wore sunglasses. I don't know if it is some sort of Norwegian seaman status symbol, but they took that blinding glare on the water and the ice without any seeming ill effect. True, they all had a fine network of squint wrinkles, and they habitually narrowed their eyes, but other than Hansen none even needed glasses for reading. I cannot explain it. Without sunglasses I would have been in serious trouble, as I spent most of my time on deck watching the sea birds.

The birds were Svalbard. They were its population, its

action, its sound, and they were everywhere. Not in vast flocks, but no matter where we were, there always was a bird of some kind, and usually one that I did not know. Summer was the time to see the sea birds, for now many unusual species rarely seen in one place gathered here far from man to breed, then left before winter to migrate to many southern locations.

I counted over twenty species of gulls, usually dominated by the twenty-eight-inch glaucous. Now as we passed the ice there was one landing with its usual clumsy belly flop near a floe that was glowing as if blue lights were buried in it. These were the monster gulls I had seen at Longyearbyen and wondered about. The captain had identified them earlier.

As this big bird came splashing in, the captain said, "I see that gull once take an eleven-inch golden plover right out of the air and swallow it whole."

I was surprised also to see the familiar herring gull in these remote waters, the white, pearl-mantled bird that does so well near civilization that New York City has its resident population, the gull almost a symbol of the sea in the United States. Haakon Godtliebsen said that they breed in large numbers here, as they do everywhere else, and that the adult has two bright red spots under its bill. When the young are born, if they do not immediately reach up and peck that red spot the parents will let them starve to death. "Like pushing a button that says 'feed me,'" the captain said. He also remarked (as Bunting had briefly mentioned on the *Lyngen*) that although the kidneys of most marine animals and birds, even fish, are not equipped to extract and excrete as waste the salt from the blood, the gull has glands that handle this effectively. Scientists experimenting with herring gulls removed those glands above the eyes that strain excess salt from the seawater through special openings in the bill. Some birds were then placed on a salt-free-water diet, some on a high-salt-water diet. The gulls that drank fresh water did not develop new glands, the others quickly grew giants.

We discussed gulls often, for they were always in the sky somewhere, near or far, and even when you realized that they were one big flying stomach you had to admire their daily wing-ballets. The captain said that Russia claims a pink gull and had recently announced the discovery of a solid black colony on Siberia's Lake Alakul.

"I'd have to see both birds to believe it," Haakon Godtliebsen said flatly.

Bird watchers are a peculiar species all of their own. I know. I'm one of them. I haven't yet reached that point where I spend my Christmas holidays helping the Audubon Society make its bird count, and I don't plaster organizational stickers on the windshield of my car, or hide in bushes with a camera and notebook, but I find the habits, flights, and beauty of birds fascinating. I may not know all the details of a species, but the high V-flight of migrating Canada geese and their barking as they speed south in the late fall and north in the spring does make me race outdoors to see them make unequaled poetry of sight and sound.

Haakon Godtliebsen was giant strides beyond me. His specialty, of course, was sea birds and he knew them as familiars, as beings that he encountered regularly in the course of his everyday life. In addition to his own probing interest he had had ornithologists aboard who added to his fund of knowledge. And he had a memory like a bank vault. Once he deposited a fact it stayed there.

One day when we had watched a great black-backed gull come close to the *Havella*, the black on its back like a saddle, the twenty-nine-inch bird sending even a pair of glaucous gulls screaming away in terror, the captain told me that the gull had a wingspread of five and a half feet, preyed mainly on terns, and destroyed the eggs of the eider duck. "Only the jaegers and the skua aren't afraid of it," he said.

A few hours later he suddenly relieved Alf Olsen at the wheel and with a sharp turn took the *Havella* off course, heading her for some black specks on the water.

Sigurd Dal shook his head in disgust. "Birds! Once he chased a Ross's gull twenty miles."

The captain motioned to me as we neared the birds. "I saw them light. They fly like hawks. Long-tailed jaegers. Fastest of the birds, beak like a hawk. Hellish fierce. They're only twenty-one inches but like I told you, even the big gulls stay away from them."

He showed me how to identify jaegers on water, the two long nine-inch central tail feathers were held in an upright position while the bird was resting. "They fly swiftly at gulls and terns and attack them, making them drop their food. They're so fast they grab that food before it hits the water."

Once, at lunch, the captain unwittingly displayed his knowledge, telling me that only 8,580 species of birds remain out of the original 1,634,000 that once existed. He wasn't particularly interested in land birds, or for that matter, land people, and concentrated on praising sea birds. He asked me to consider that four-fifths of all living birds are made up of land birds, and that five-sevenths of the world is water. For every square mile of land there are two and a half miles of salt water. Yet sea birds make up only three percent of the world's species. That percentage includes a mere 260 species, with just one dozen families.

It wouldn't have surprised me if the captain named every species. He didn't. Mainly he commented on what we saw. He was happy to have a fellow bird watcher aboard. It might even have helped make up for some of my shortcomings as a seaman.

I got to the point where the passing of some days was

marked by a new bird I saw. One day was memorable when I was the first to spot a small gull with a rosy tinge on its white feathers. It was flying with some black-capped terns. Soon three more appeared in the sky.

"Ross's gull!" the captain said, immediately leaving the wheel spinning, Olsen running to grab it. "We don't see them often. Most naturalists never see one. Mystery birds. They don't go south. Breed in eastern Siberia then fly north over the Polar Sea. No one knows where they are between October and June."

They lit on the water among the black-capped terns, a pure, delicate white, the pink markings making them look wounded.

Often birds came toward the *Havella* and landed on the water near us, then would suddenly take off and vanish. Why they approached was something not even the captain could explain. "Curiosity, hunger?" He shook his head. "This is a lonely place. Maybe they just want to take a look at us."

Haakon Godtliebsen identified gulls that I thought I would never see except in a bird book—Fork-tails darting like monstrous swallows, Franklin's Rosy, Sabine's, the Point Barrow, the little Black-headed, the Mew, the Rosy or Wedge-winged. The elegant white sixteen-inch Kittiwakes, also gulls, would appear in flocks overhead as suddenly as a snowstorm, crying *kitta-aa, kitta-aa,* flaking all around the boat. Razorbills, fulmars, auks, old squaws, murres, were near us often.

The two species we saw most often sometimes appeared at the same time; one, about eight inches long, the black and white dovekie always came in flocks, flying like quail, landing near the boat, diving beneath the water, using their wings like oars to propel them underwater. The other, the black guillemot, was about twice the dovekie's size with a long bill, sooty black, with white markings and bright red feet. Trim, compact, it looked like a big dove. The captain called it the "sea pigeon." It rested buoyantly on the water very near us, not diving as often as the dovekie. Haakon Godtliebsen liked the guillemot, saying that they were the last birds to fly south, staying on the sea until it is almost completely icebound.

Arctic terns flew overhead but rarely stopped, their flight as swift as the wind that suddenly sprang up bringing them. The captain told me they were the champion migrators; one banded Arctic tern flew from Labrador to Natal, South Africa, covering nine thousand miles in three months and twenty-two days.

Clown-headed puffins came bursting upon us like a troupe of medieval jesters, with their white breasts, stark black wings and backs, grotesquely broad beaks slashed with brilliant red, purple, and yellow cross-stripes.

These large-billed puffins, found only in this region, could hold several small fish side by side in that huge bill. I saw one puffin go underwater like a stone, then come up with so many small fish in its broad bill that it looked like the fish were catching the bird. After the summer nesting season the bright colors of that bill are shed in nine separate strips. It seemed a strange bird to be here, looking as tropical as an African parrot, which was what the captain called it, the "sea parrot."

He said it dove deep where the heavy salt water subjected it to powerful pressure. But it has a buckler that protects its vital organs: across the lower portion of the breast a flat plate of bone and cartilage covers the abdomen. They were real sea birds, the captain said, spending much of the summer feeding and sleeping on the water, going to land only to breed.

The Arctic petrel was the main performer. Smoky, grayish-white, chunky, its long, tapered sail-plane wings kept it gliding just above the waves for long periods without visible motion of the wings. Sounds of harsh growling, almost like angry dogs, heralded the approach of these storm birds. They would land near the boat, then take off, seemingly with a long walk across the water, as the Apostle Peter is said to have done, and from whom the birds got their name, *petrellus*, little Peter. The captain called the petrel's effortless flight dynamic soaring. They rose against the wind from a level where it was slowed by the friction of the waves, to a higher level where it blew faster. The petrel then glided downwind to gain momentum to soar again, often disappearing into the sun.

That constant sun merged time into one big day. We had no tight schedule, and as there was no night there was no hurry. Wherever humanity herds in the clutter called civilization, we are governed by the timeless rising and setting of the sun. Our lives are attuned to it. In this polar region where there are few men, that pattern is weirdly distorted. In the winter, as Bolin had described, the sun does not rise at all, night blends into night. In summer, the sun not only never sets, dusk immediately becomes dawn.

At 5:27 A.M. the sun was well above the horizon, and continued to rise until it reached its zenith at high noon, as it does everywhere. At twenty-seven minutes past midnight it was at its lowest point, hanging like a flaming torch just above the horizon, still spraying daylight at us. Then it started its rise again, shining high and bright at 4:27 A.M.

I suppose one could get used to that inescapable bright eye lighting up the hours normally welcomed in darkness, the romantic time, the cocktail-sun-over-the-yardarm hour, night coming down to mask and dull the trials and defeats of the hard day. I like the sun, but I also like the moon and the stars, and quiet dusk when the harshnesses of the day are softened, and the world seems to hold still for a while. There is, for me, at least, something psychologically pleasing about dusk, even in the word itself, a time when I slow down, clear my mind, and begin to look forward to the new day ahead that will always make everything all right. So, although I appreciated the novelty of that eerie ubiquity of the sun, never quite believing that it was not going to go down and give the moon a chance, I didn't enjoy it the same way the crew did.

They hadn't seen the sun all winter, so they wallowed in it like desert animals discovering oasis water. They sunbathed, they continually washed clothing, hanging it in the sun to dry, clothing that I am certain never got so much soap-and-water attention other times. They stood at the rail and dreamed at the sun, they ran hands through their hair, washing the sun into their heads. And they, like me, slept little, other than catnapping, seemingly feeling that if they kept their eyes closed too long the sun might go away.

My pencilings of that phenomenon have the sun traveling in an arc, shaped somewhat like a rainbow, surging up from its lowest niche pretty well above the horizon on the left until, in gradual elevations, it reached noon, then, in stages, going down again to almost touch the horizon at midnight—then forming the rising arc all over again.

To me, the sun seemed to go up and down in waves, almost like the motion of the sea. Actually, it moved on a flat, somewhat tilted plane, lying highest above the horizon in the south, at the lowest in the north. It was an illusion, I knew, due to the earth's turning, its rotation and revolution and the fixed tilt of its axis in space. But knowing this didn't lessen the strangeness of the sun's constant presence.

It was as if I had suddenly reached the ends of the earth itself, and, in fact, here I literally had. But the earth still rotated on a north-south axis once every twenty-four hours. That axis, however, was not exactly perpendicular to the flat plane on which the earth moved. It was tilted almost twenty-four degrees. That tilt was the Midnight Sun trick. We were actually leaning toward the sun, with this North Pole region getting it all, leaving the South Pole in complete darkness.

9

A touch on the wheel and she responded like a horse to a rein. I didn't delude myself into thinking that Haakon Godtliebsen had placed the safety of *Havella* and the lives of the crew in my hands when he occasionally let me handle the ketch. And no one said ketch; it was "her" or "she" or *Havella*, a personality, and the trim craft was that, a delight to handle, as I discovered after four or five instructional sessions with the captain. There was no traffic here; we were the only ship, the only people for many miles. So when I was at the helm there was nothing but water ahead, sometimes some small ice, but nothing that could get me into trouble. I could get off course a bit; it takes a seasoned man at the wheel to keep rigidly on course. It's a matter of coordination of eye, hand, and wheel that only experience can bring together.

When I took the *Havella* across the vast open water ahead, the sky incredibly blue, the ice pack in the distance gleaming a pale pink on the horizon, the sea running smooth beneath us, I saw, and felt, how one could become so attached to this way of life that he could never do anything else. I understood how the silence attracted Aage Rutwold, and got the feel of the freedom that the crew of the *Havella* had. They worked for a shipowner in Tromsø who rarely bothered them when they were out on charter, and they spent all of the good months on this uncluttered sea. Out here in the *Havella* you owned the world. There was no clock ticking in your head to tell you that you had to do this, or couldn't do that. There was this feeling of actually being free and flying, as Olsen had put it just before we left King's Bay.

The islands we passed were far enough away not to cause trouble with ice and shallow, treacherous water, but they were close enough to impress you with their majesty. Ice covered most of them like silver foil.

For the first time in my life I no longer even counted the days, and knew what the approximate hour was only when Aage announced breakfast, lunch, or dinner.

Those meals became whatever timetable there was. The day we had the fish pudding, light as a French soufflé; the night Aage sliced the *fenalår* he had been saving, the bitey, delicious, salted, smoked mutton; the supper with *puss pass*, also mutton with cabbage, carrots, and potatoes; the afternoon we had the Norwegian favorite, *kabaret*, an aspic of cod tongues, and the hour when Aage came beaming with pride and served *kalvefilet med sur fløte*, sautéed scallops of veal with a sour cream sauce thickened with shredded goat cheese.

There was one day, however, that I will never need anything, meal or man, to prod alive out of memory. It's always there.

I was alone at the wheel, the crew for various reasons were below, and the *Havella* went smooth as silk across quiet water. I held steady on course, dead north, for about an hour when the flashings began, a steady bright blinking from the shoreline of one of the distant islands. There was repeated bright flash after flash like SOS signals. Could there be someone else out there in trouble?

I was ready to call below when Alf Olsen stuck his head out of the hatchway, checking on me. I told him about the flashes.

"We're heading due north," he said. "Those are iceblinks. Reflections from the wall of ice on the far horizon." He went below again. Why hadn't I noticed the iceblinks before? Were we getting closer to the island glaciers?

Clouds moved in veiling the sun, the sky darkened, and fog came drifting on an offshore breeze like smoke from a forest fire, shredding and floating, making vision poor. We were encountering more fog every day now. The temperature was staying well above freezing most of the time, dropping when the sun rimmed the horizon, then rising again as it rose. Sometimes fog was the result.

Without warning, it happened.

Through a break in a drift of fog directly ahead, a wall of ice towered, as suddenly as if dropped from the sky.

I stared in disbelief, hands locked on the wheel. My yell for the captain brought him clumping up.

We closed with the ice blockade, moving fast.

Fog swirled over the iceberg, then lifted, forming a circle around it. It was a shiny gray-green monster lifting pronged horns of ice, so large that the only way to avoid it would be to hop over its humped back.

"Hold it steady," the captain said quietly, not offering to take the wheel. He couldn't have anyway. My hands were frozen tight to it. I doubted that even the upcoming crash against the ice that was obviously coming could break my grip.

Abruptly, the iceberg, dead ahead of me, vanished.

Haakon Godtliebsen gently pulled my fingers from the wheel.

"Mirage," he said quietly, explaining that it was what is

called a looming mirage, caused by an abrupt temperature change. He said that the "loom" happened often this time of year and sometimes made navigation difficult.

Relieving my embarrassment somewhat, Sigurd Dal said that you had to see several looms before you could tell which was a mirage and which was real ice.

Then, seeing ice that size head on, mirage was just a word. I have since learned that far more seasoned travelers and astute observers have been deceived on a much grander scale.

On a 1906 Arctic expedition, Admiral Robert E. Peary reported seeing a new land mass at a distance, which he located on charts and named Crocker Land. Excited, the American Museum of Natural History spent $300,000 assembling and outfitting an expedition under arctic veteran Donald MacMillan to explore Crocker Land. MacMillan had bad luck. Wrecking his ship, traveling on foot over the ice, he went even beyond where Crocker Land was supposed to be to find only empty ocean. Discouraged, suspecting that it may have been a mirage Peary saw, but still impressed with the admiral's experience, at great hardship MacMillan and his men made their way back to the point where the Peary expedition had first sighted Crocker Land. It was a clear day. There was nothing where Peary had said the new land had been sighted. But far west, vivid in a burst of sunlight, the mountains of Crocker Land loomed. Again on foot, the MacMillan party made for it, the snow-capped mountains clear, perfect before them. As the men moved, so did the mountains, the mirage melting before their eyes. Two veteran arctic explorers had been completely duped.

Mesmeric in their reality, mirages can convince an entire community, and with one sweep take in a collection of trained observers. The population of Whitehorse, Yukon, awoke one morning to find that overnight a huge new mountain had appeared a few miles away. As they excitedly rushed toward it, the mountain disappeared. Whitehorse had a job convincing visitors that the whole place hadn't been on a tremendous binge.

An alert photographer in Debreczen, Hungary, not far from Budapest, preserved his community's veracity by taking clear pictures of church steeples and villages suddenly growing out of the sky, complete with the landscaping of giant trees and shimmering lakes, plus, where no tracks existed, a line of railroad cars rushing along the horizon.

In 1958, the Italian navy (that considers the Mediterranean its own private lake) proudly announced that it had discovered a new island rising from the mists and sent a ship to explore it. They arrived, red-faced, to find the mist still there, but the island had vanished.

Even students of mirages can be taken in. Enos A. Mills, who had encountered many and wrote of them in an article, "Mapping Mirages," saw what he called a mirage masterpiece, a herd of cattle grazing on a not too distant hill. He had just traveled from that direction and knew that the herd wasn't really there, but many miles away. Convinced that the mirage was actually mirroring cattle, Mills and his party were hoping for fresh beef, even if it was several days in coming. Astounded, they watched one "steer" pick up another in its mouth, another fall off a cliff, bounce, then get up and join the rest of the herd. Later they found the mirage was projecting an anthill!

Famed explorer Roy Chapman Andrews (who had seen many a mirage), moving through an unknown area of the Gobi Desert, saw a blue lake stretching before him, beside it a green island, birds flying over the water. He had one of his men, a topographer, sketch the lake while he investigated. As he neared, the lake blurred, the island wiggled, then vanished. When he reached the "lake" it was a sandy stretch, the birds, a herd of antelope. "All but their heads," the explorer said, "were obscured in a stratum of shimmering heat waves on the sand." He returned to the topographer, busily sketching the lake (still there, sparkling in the sunlight), who wouldn't believe it was a mirage.

The mirage mirror is sometimes not unlike those in a carnival Fun House that, with a turn of position, throw back a grinning twin image, convert a skinny man into a monster and an overweight woman into a ninety-pound fashion model.

It is not uncommon for a mirage to take a ship, split it in two and sail the halves in opposite directions. The surviving members of Scott's arctic expedition, awaiting arrival of their rescue ship, *Terra Nova*, saw it coming for them as a pair of ships, one upside down, the other above it, moving toward them across the skyline. The real ship was invisible thirty miles away.

Watching for his father's ship to appear, arctic navigator William Scoresby, Jr., saw it coming for him through the sky wrong side up, so real that with binoculars he made out details of masts and hull. The actual ship was moving in normal fashion thirty-four miles away, fifteen miles beyond the horizon.

Splitting a single ship or sending it topsy-turvy through the air is barely flexing a mirage muscle. During the Crimean War, the entire British Fleet, inverted, was seen sailing home through the sky. To convince the population that they hadn't lost their minds, the *Illustrated London News* explained and published a photograph of the incredible sight. The famous mirage vision of Hastings was recalled, when during the hot summer of 1798 the French coast from Calais to Dieppe was in clear view for three hours, an unviewable distance of fifty miles from the English beach. The same century that the British Fleet was treated so ignominiously, a mirage hung the night-lighted city of Paris, upended, in the heavens. Sometime after that, the magic mirror pulled off even a trickier stunt: it stood the Eiffel Tower on its head—on top of itself.

America's most famous mirage presaged tragedy: in 1878, when General Custer marched his army from Fort Abraham

Lincoln to do battle at Little Big Horn, the farewell party stood waving until the soldiers vanished along the trail. Later, when the people returned to the fort, Custer and his men reappeared, a ghost army marching through the sky.

Mirage, a French word, from *mirer,* to look at, or *se mirer,* to be reflected, was added to the world's vocabulary by Gaspard Monge, a French physicist who accompanied Napoleon and his army when they invaded Egypt in 1798. Visions of lakes, lush gardens, and rosy minarets kept appearing on the desert before the troops, sending them to their knees in prayer. But not Monge, who realized that somehow an intermingling of hot and cold air was responsible for the wraithlike sights.

Although it is deluding oneself to try to put the enigma of the mirage simply, it is an optical illusion caused by refraction of light penetrating layers of atmosphere of different density. Our modern Monge, James H. Gordon, studied mirages when he retired from the United States Weather Bureau, saw several and talked with others who had, and made so much sense from the mystery that his findings were included in the 1959 annual report of the Smithsonian Institution. He observes: "The widespread belief that a mirage is something unreal, a sort of trick played on the eyes, is wrong. The picture a mirage presents is real but never quite accurate. The effect of a mirage is to change the seeming location or appearance of an object—not infrequently, both. The seeming shift in position may be hardly noticeable or may amount to many miles, change in appearance may be slight or extensive. Both changes are brought about by refraction: a bending in the course of the light path from object to observer which occurs when light passes from dense to less dense air, or the reverse."

An example of refraction most of us have observed is a spoon in a glass of water, or a swimmer standing in water. From an angle, the spoon handle seems to bend where it enters the water—so do the bather's legs—an optical illusion resulting from the great difference in densities of air and water. For mirage making, a mass of air must also have a progressive, unusual density change within it, the reason more mirages are seen on deserts and in polar regions such as Svalbard. Gordon suggests that the function of such an air mass as a refraction or "bending" agency is similar to the lenses in optical instruments.

The air lens depth may vary from mere inches to more than a hundred feet, its area from several square feet to square miles. Gordon places mirages in two categories: No. 1 Lens, and No. 2 Lens. No. 1 is denser at the top than at the bottom, making an object appear lower than it is. For example, cobalt sky, near the horizon can appear on the road, or dry land, as blue water. No. 2 is denser at the bottom, making an object seem higher than it is, resulting in three effects:

(a) If the air lens is on a rise between object and viewer, a clear picture of something that normally would be invisible behind that ridge is brought into sight by the mirage.

(b) When the air lens is in the temperature inversion layer of atmosphere, ranging from a few feet to thousands above the ground, the object is distorted, in addition to being lifted.

(c) If the air lens is in the temperature inversion layer, an image can be lifted and shown, a few miles, or hundreds of miles away, upright or inverted, frequently both.

The two air lenses create mirages this way: No. 1 is formed by a superheated ground surface raising the temperature of the air immediately above the ground, reversing the usual decrease of temperature and density with altitude, thus the water mirage on the highway many of us have seen. Lens No. 2 forms over a cold ground surface, often when a temperature trend reversal quickens the rate of density decreases. This is the lens that picks up a hidden building, city, or a mountain and lifts it into sight.

Scientific study largely agrees with Mr. Gordon. R. W. Wood created mirages in his laboratory by heating slabs of slate.

Scientists, however, refer to mirages as types. Their *inferior* mirage is Gordon's simple Lens 1; *superior*, his Lens 2. *Superior* is sometimes called *looming* (the one that tricked Admiral Peary— and me) and also explains the famous *Brockengespenst*, the specter of the Brocken, a giant shadow named for Brocken Hill in the German Harz mountains. A mountain climber looks up, frightened, to behold a huge figure against the mountain that moves as he moves. The colossal mocking shadow is caused by reflection and diffraction of light from the moisture in mist, where the shadow of the observer is cast onto a cloud bank and loomed. The *lateral* mirage (two layers of air separated by a vertical plane) is the double illusion, two identical ships, sometimes sailing in opposite directions, or an image hidden around the corner of a mountain being brought into sight. The *towering* mirage pulls objects into fantastic lengths (the ants that looked like cattle).

Mirage effects, however, are really not all mathematically that simple. After years of study, James Gordon still has an unanswered question: "How is energy, in the form of the light carrying the picture or image, conveyed through the atmosphere for great distances with no apparent loss of potential? The city that looms so large has not been magnified by any telescopic effect. As nearly as we can judge, it simply fails to get smaller with distance as one would expect, according to the laws of physics. Its light power fades little if any, which seems to present an irrational situation."

If that perplexing mirage problem remains, another modern mystery has been scientifically solved—by mirages. The flying saucers that have puzzled and intrigued Americans, causing many scares and some panic, are apparently not strange aircraft from another planet after all. According to Dr. Donald H. Menzel, Professor of Astrophysics, Harvard University, flying saucers are indeed "as real as rainbows." So are mirages. Dr. Menzel is certain that the more unusual types of mirages are the mysterious crafts from outer space. He explains (and has proved with laboratory tests, using chemicals of different weights and projected beams of light) that overhead warm air slants downward the lights from autos and streetlights, creating the bright space discs that appear to sweep quickly across a night sky. This is caused by the abnormal condition of layers of warm air *over* colder air, "inversions." Dr. Menzel thus explains the noted Lubbock lights of Texas (that began a flying saucer debate) as the images of a string of lights at a distance, or the reduplicated images of one extremely bright light.

Dr. Menzel also considers a mirage an image caused by a lens of air and says that where the usual daytime mirage projects the picture of the sky against the earth, the nighttime desert mirage throws the image of the earth against the sky. If there are distant city lights, atmospheric conditions being right, lights will appear in the sky. If the air is turbulent, the lights will seem to be moving, sometimes rapidly. He explains daytime flying saucers as sunlight reflected from dust, smoke, haze, collected high in the atmosphere in an inversion haze. Again, turbulence makes the trapped and reflected light mirages move like mysterious spacecraft.

What happens if mirage types mix? A spectacular is born, the most famous, the Fata Morgana, created by a mystic blend of *inferior* and *superior* mirages. Occurring over the Strait of Messina, between Sicily and the tip of the Italian boot, sometimes appearing as an oriental city in the sea, it was named for Morgan La Fay, legendary evil fairy sister of King Arthur, and is the best known of all mirages. Some scientists believe that it is merely the distorted vision of the nearby city of Messina. Whatever the explanation, it has appeared in both sea and sky, complete with castles, turreted buildings, a medieval city with gardens, herds of animals, men on foot and horseback.

Even if I had known all of this in Svalbard, I doubt that it would have made much difference.

When a mirage picks up a giant iceberg and dumps it dead ahead of you, no scientific fact can explain away its stark and frightening reality.

And real it was. As the captain pried my hands off the wheel, he said that the same thing had happened to him and that later he had seen the actual iceberg up close.

"You will too," he said. "It's there, where we're going."

10

At a distance, from our vantage point in the sea miles from them, the icy islands sparkled in the sun like a great looping necklace of rock crystal. The archipelago rose out of the Arctic Ocean to our right, the captain marking our progress for me on his chart, drawing a line of ink along the islands as we passed them. He didn't draw the line all the way to our destination. He charted as we went, not as we hoped to go; final direction would be determined by water and ice conditions.

The chart focused just on the Svalbard area, and for the first time the size of the island group lay clear before me, emphasizing the fact that this mountainous chain actually was larger than Belgium. This was an entire wild country floating out here in a sea that prompted repeated warnings on the chart, "NOTICE. The soundings east of Amsterdamöya are mostly uncertain. Great care should be exercised in these waters."

The chart was prepared by the Norway Polar Institute in Norwegian, so some of the names were confusing. We had come out of King's Bay and swung abruptly right when we left the fjord, passing James I Land, Haakon VII Land, Albert I Land, and Andrée Land. This last was named for the Swedish scientist Salomon August Andrée, who tried to reach the Pole by balloon and was found dead on the island which was named for him.

This reminded me that right now I had made it closer to the North Pole than many of the explorers. I asked the captain about Andrée and, surprising me, he said that he didn't know much about him except that he wasn't Norwegian and therefore hadn't made much sense. Andrée knew little about flying a balloon and took two men with him who knew nothing at all about it. The three men also were completely ignorant of polar conditions.

"Their bodies were found thirty-three years after they disappeared," Haakon Godtliebsen said. "On the southwest side of that island, which was called White Island then."

He expounded briefly on the fact that most of the men who were lost trying to reach the Pole hadn't properly prepared themselves for the north. They didn't know how to live on pack ice and survive, didn't know enough about the polar sea and navigation, hadn't studied weather conditions. Andrée, for example, didn't even know the direction of the prevailing polar winds which would propel his balloon. He thought there was a constant wind from the south in the summer. There wasn't.

Each large island we passed was gouged by fjords. They ran out from the sea like small rivers, leaving a trail of smoky-blue water, each one calling to me to follow as it cut its way ashore. Later we would travel up two of these isolated fjords. I understand that many get that same luring call from these mysterious streams that flow between mountains. Following fjords has become big business in Norway, and nowhere else except there and Svalbard do they appear in such abundance. One in Norway, Sogne fjord, is one hundred miles long, four thousand feet deep and ships sail its length. Its sides rise five thousand feet. Their numbers here didn't lessen their fascination

—each appeared to have a different shape and personality. These sea lochs, formed by glaciers or by a fault in the earth, or by both, differ from river estuaries in that their channels are long, straight, and narrow, with very steep parallel sides that plunge far below the water level. Most fjords are shallow at the mouth, then become deep as they move inland. These of Svalbard gave the impression of the sea slicing straight through rock. The fjords we had entered at Longyearbyen and King's Bay seemed calm inlet approaches to a harbor; these runaway bodies of seawater savagely slashed their way between steep cliffs. Viking water raiding from the sea.

Many small islands broke up whatever coastline there was into a jumbled mass of rock and ice. We were staying to the north of Svalbard and would continue our sharp right-angle swing and pass two more large islands, Ny Fries Land and Gustav V Land, and at least a half dozen smaller islands before we reached our destination, Nordaustlandet, the second largest island in the group and the most inaccessible.

That island jutted out from the far northern section dwarfing everything around it except the sea. The chart didn't show the ice astride it, but fjords were clearly marked and so were the mountains.

The captain didn't use his pen on this sector of his map of the sea, but ran a blunt forefinger along the water near the edge of the island, taking me past it and looping the finger into a fjord, then back into the interior of the island.

"That's it," he said. "I'll tell you more about the place we're going as we get closer."

I went back on deck. The water was calm; gulls were over Andrée's Island floating on thermals, so motionless they looked painted against the shoreline.

From a distance the objects that suddenly appeared off our bow looked like white Sunfish-size sailboats about to capsize. As the wind swept them closer they became flat ice covered with snow. I wasn't sure what they were until the captain stopped the *Havella* and Olsen nimbly went down a rope ladder on the side and hopped onto an ice cake. He came back aboard with a large bucket of chopped ice.

Freshwater ice. Calves from a glacier. Icebergs. Gresswell's Ice Age. We were near the islands on which the ice caps sat like a big man riding a small donkey.

The snowy bergs didn't arrive in flotillas, but we did see about a dozen most of the time now. It was ice that didn't cause any problem, for it could be seen in the bright sunlight hundreds of yards ahead. Haakon Godtliebsen avoided the icebergs with an easy turn of the wrist.

Black specks on some of them became seals that slid smoothly off, disappearing as we drew closer. Occasionally I'd look behind to see the seal surface and follow us for a short time, in and out of the water like a porpoise.

Suddenly a black head would pop up in our wake, then the sleek body. I had realized that seals were skillful swimmers but had never seen a wild one in action before, flashing through the water like a big, fast fish. As this was a boatful of seal experts, I soon knew a thing or two about those animals.

I didn't try to dig any deeper into the sealing industry than I had in my first talk with Olsen. It was still a respectable industry in Norway as no one had yet banned the selling and wearing of sealskin coats, and out on wild water in the Arctic Ocean with five Norwegians, all of whom had been sealers, was not the place to get into a discussion on the merits and the cruelties of hunting seals, if, indeed, there were any. I was enough of a realist to know that no one cried "foul" at the slaughter of sheep, lambs, cattle, calves, pigs, goats, rabbits, chickens, turkeys, even horses, and no one had ever complained about the Orientals killing thousands of dogs annually for their kitchen pots.

Thinking about that I recalled that the ancient seamen had believed that seals were half dog and half fish, and I could understand why as I watched ringed seals sometimes frolicking like puppies in our wake.

One day the captain cut the motor and drifted up on a ringed seal asleep on the sunlit sea off our starboard.

It was lying motionless, floating, flippers hugged close to its body, its head underwater, its back humped above. We timed that nap at five minutes. Suddenly, as if by some signal, it lifted its head and nose out of the water, took several fast breaths, then nodded off again, peaceful as a cat on a stool before a fireplace, its head sinking again into the sea as it continued napping.

Haakon Godtliebsen remembered a Danish scientist claiming that when seals slept they were able to quickly lower the rate of their heartbeat from one hundred a minute to less than twenty. "Resting their hearts as well as their bodies," the captain said enviously.

This was the principal animal of the Arctic and had a wide distribution. There were six types in the north, but just two in these waters, the ringed and the bearded. We saw mostly ringed seals, not hundreds, but enough to know that we were in their territory.

There are two families of these unique animals. Eared Seals, and Earless or "true" Seals, with just two Eared species, the fur seal and the sea lion.

Earless seals hear very well. There are small channels or canals that go to the inner ear which close when the seal dives underwater (as do the openings behind the nostrils) and open when he surfaces.

The crew claimed that through various observations and tests they knew that at least the ringed seal could see well underwater and also hear, even with the canal to the inner ear closed. The seals had been seen catching polar cod in deep, clear water, and had often gotten out of the way of the *Havella*, even when the animals' backs were toward the ship. Once Olsen had seen a submerged ringed seal veer quickly away when he had fired a shot at a duck flying just above the surface of the water.

To me the seal's limbs seemed to turn backward, and weren't really limbs at all but flippers, fin feet. It didn't seem possible that they could move on land at all, but the crew claimed that they could. They seemed to slide along on their stomachs, using a back-humping motion like a caterpillar, moving by front and rear contractions of the body. I observed that tortuous but fast action when a ringed seal saw us and humped from the center of a large ice floe to get into the water.

Adult ringed seals are about five feet long and average 160 pounds, with the females shorter and one quarter lighter in weight. Darkish brown, the fur paling to yellow underneath, when just out of water they gleamed like buffed metal.

This wasn't the breeding season; it was the loafing season. Whenever we saw a seal he was basking in the sun, on the ice or in the water. They're polygamous, breeding again soon after the female has weaned her pups a few weeks after they are born in March. Olsen said the mating in the sea was an agile and acrobatic affair. The male mated with all of the females that would accept him and took no parental responsibility.

In early March before the pups are born the female is ballooned with fat, sheathed in blubber up to two and a half inches thick. A seal with this amount of fat can lie on the ice without leaving a sign, no tell-tale trace of body heat. For its skin temperature is just above the freezing point, while its internal temperature is 99.2° F. Restricted surface circulation permits just enough blood to pump to the skin to keep it from freezing. Thus, as heat dissipation is minimized, no increase in the metabolic rate is needed to produce heat, whether seals are on ice or in freezing water.

When the pup is born in March, it is immediately licked dry by the mother. Instantly the offspring begins bleating. At this moment, the sound and the scent of her pup are imprinted upon the female's memory, enabling her to identify her pup from all of the others born all around her on ice floes.

Ringed seals don't always whelp on ice floes. Sometimes their young are born in a six-foot-long burrow dug in snow by the claws on the female's front flippers. That burrow, ending in a tiny igloo, extends to the breathing hole in the ice.

In winter these breathing holes, with a single seal having as many as five, a mile apart, are also escape hatches. A seal usually remains underwater seven to nine minutes, surfacing at the breathing hole for forty-five seconds to get oxygen. Olsen told me he timed one ringed seal that remained under for twenty minutes. These life-giving breathing holes in the ice are found in small openings in fjord ice or land-fast ice, or dug with clawed front flippers in ice between floes that have been weakened as the result of floes grinding against one another.

That floating ice is a dangerous nursery. Moving with the current, the floes not only grind together, but in the heavy swells of the sea heave six feet out of the water. Storms flip the floes atop one another, crack them, and push them up into masses of pressure ridges.

Females can escape through the breathing holes or natural openings in the ice, but often the helpless pups perish on the floes.

But without storms and a raging sea, the pups prosper. Their mother's milk is very rich, containing 42.6 percent fat and 10.4 percent protein. Feeding from the female's two teats several times a day, the young triple their weight in two weeks, then are weaned.

In contrast, the mother rapidly loses as much as 50 percent of her weight. Courting and mating are strenuous activities, her hair moults soon after she has the pup, and mainly, she fasts while nursing her young one, not having time for her fishing chores.

The weaned pups, fat as pigs, encased in blubber three inches thick, live off that fat for about two weeks, drifting aimlessly on ice floes. When the fat is gone they begin feeding on the tiny crustaceans that swarm in arctic waters in late spring and summer. These pups are solitary, but as they reach a year of age they join the adults.

Enemies are men, polar bears, and killer whales. The ringed seal used to be the very basis of existence for the Eskimo, providing him with food and shelter, even heat from its blubber, which was burned. But now that the Eskimo has advanced the seal is no longer important to his way of life.

The ringed isn't prized for its hide, and isn't preyed upon by man as much as the other species such as the harp, the hooded, and the hair seals.

We didn't see a half dozen of the other species native to these waters, the bearded seal. It is one of the largest, the males reaching ten feet, weighing as much as eight hundred pounds. Tufts of white bristle growing on each side of its muzzle gave it the name. These are solitary animals, except during mating season, when sometimes they can be seen in small herds. They prefer ice floes not far from land, usually don't make their own breathing holes, but use leads and natural openings in the ice. The captain told me their skin was the thickest of all seals and good for making sole leather, and once was used for harpoon lines, which not only had to be very strong but flexible. The bearded seal's skin also was used for tent coverings and for making skin boats, *umiaks*. Progress is this seal's friend.

Of the seal's three enemies the crew seemed fascinated by the killer whale, telling me that the remains of fourteen seals had been found in the stomach of one twenty-four-foot killer.

They said that killer whales spot seals on ice floes, swim to them, raise their great heads out of the water, prop them on the ice, spilling the seal into their jaws, which open wide enough to gulp an entire seal.

The dorsal fin, projecting six feet out of the water like a sail, is the killer's identification mark in the sea. Their bodies are jet black, marked with streaks of white and yellow, and they travel and attack in packs.

Killer whales have been seen attacking a huge baleen whale many times their size. They darted in tearing at the tail flukes and flippers until the wounded whale dropped its tongue out. Then the killers tore out the tongue and ate it and the lips, leaving the whale to die.

On one of Captain Falcon Scott's arctic expeditions he told of killer whales that had seen two of his sled dogs on an ice floe. They came up under the floe, battering it into splinters with their heads.

The captain talked about a killer whale caught in the Bering Sea that had thirty-two baby seals in its stomach, and said that these thirty-foot creatures had teeth like a shark's and were hated by all fishermen because they ripped up nets to get at the trapped fish.

I had no idea that there was a monster like this in these waters and looked with new respect at the seals sunning on ice floes.

One afternoon we came up slowly on a flat floe the size of a barn roof. A big fat seal was sound asleep in its center. He didn't even lift his head as we approached and the captain cut the engine, perhaps one hundred yards from the floe.

Alf Olsen looked at the seal, said, "A fat lazy one, just what we need," went below and came up with a scoped rifle.

Thinking of killer whales and borrowed time, I said, "Look, Alf, you aren't going to shoot that seal I hope."

He gave me a puzzled look and said that the captain thought that what they were going to do would interest me very much.

"Shooting the seal is only one part of it," he said. "Small part."

If puzzlement was involved with what the captain thought would interest me, then we were off to a good start.

Alf studied the seal again through the rifle scope, then went to the rail and put the rifle to his shoulder, carefully sighting in on the animal, holding it for a long time without a tremor.

Sigurd Dal came over to stand beside me, telling me that the shot must be exact, to the heart or the brain, killing the seal instantly, for if it slid off the floe it would immediately sink and be lost.

With the sharp crack of the rifle, the seal lifted slightly, then fell back. It was a difficult offhand shot, but the feeling that I had, knowing that this was supposed to be part of creating entertainment for me, was something less than admiration for Olsen's shooting skill. I hadn't come all this way to watch something harmless be killed, but to view an area that was free from this human arrogance.

Haakon Godtliebsen headed for the floe, spinning the *Havella* to its edge.

Blood danced across the ice, pink and dark red lines spider-webbing from the seal. Olsen threw the rope ladder over the side, went down it, and jumped onto the floe, easily carrying the seal back on his shoulder.

It lay on the deck four feet long, its brown-yellow pelt dotted with dark circular spots ringed with lighter color that gave the ringed seal its name. I reached over to touch it, to see if the fur was as velvety as it looked.

Olsen stopped me. "Don't touch it until I have a good look. You could get *spekk*-finger—"

He took the knife from his belt scabbard and carefully touched the skin of the seal, going over it inch by inch.

While he made his examination, Sigurd Dal told me about *spekk*-finger.

It's the Norwegian name for a finger infection common among sealers, and it is not unusual for over ten percent of an entire sealing fleet to contract it. The sealing industry fears it, since the disease makes it impossible for a sealer to work for several weeks, and the men are often infected at the height of the sealing season.

It is picked up while handling the seal, skinning it, or removing its blubber. The infected finger swells quickly and is extremely painful. The skin of the finger becomes red and taut, the severe pain increases and the other joints in the hand stiffen. It leaves permanent damage to the finger bones.

Dal had seen cases where the pain was so intense that the sealer amputated his own finger.

The cause isn't certain, but Dal said that study has proved that the infection usually resulted after handling older seals with infected wounds, or scars and abscesses in their subcutaneous tissues.

In severe cases it used to be necessary to amputate *spekk* fingers, but today, if treated quickly enough, aureomycin removes the infection.

Finally satisfied that this was a safe seal, Olsen deftly skinned it, peeling the fur back like a glove. The captain got the *Havella* under way again, heading her toward the shoreline, misty in haze. Sigurd Dal went forward to his usual position in the bow. As we drew closer to the shore, its rocky, snow-covered mountains elevated out of the haze.

Alf Olsen was stripping off the white seal blubber and cutting it in pieces. Aage Rutwold appeared with a pail of burning charcoal. He sat it on the deck, capped it with a wire screen and began barbecuing the seal fat.

It didn't have the aroma of sirloin on the backyard grill; it was strong, fishy, and it stayed in the nostrils until the wind shifted, taking the smoke from the sizzling blubber shoreward.

Dal suddenly shouted to the captain, who took the *Havella* in a right turn toward the island, then cut the engine as a large floe appeared dead ahead. Hansen went to get the anchor. With Alf helping, the two men made the *Havella* fast to the floe.

With the engine stilled, the silence came suddenly as if let off a leash, a big, loping silence, broken only by the spitting sounds of broiling blubber.

Haakon was at the rail with binoculars, watching the shore. Alf, Sigurd, Harald, and Aage took positions covering all directions. Arctic terns, the "sea swallows," with red beaks and silvery stomachs, went past like hurled darts.

As the Norwegians played their silent game, I remembered an explorer, perhaps Peary, who sometimes got poetic, writing that the only important sound here was the clang of a glacier calving into the sea, a bell ringing out the ages. All I could hear was the water lapping at the *Havella*, Aage cooking the seal when he returned from his station at the rail from time to time, and the creaking against the ice floe to which we were anchored. Even the gulls stitched to the sky along the shoreline were too far away to be audible. The captain remained at the rail riveted to his binoculars. There was no conversation among the crew.

"He comes!" Haakon said suddenly.

Without binoculars I couldn't see what the captain saw, and was tempted to go to him and take them, put them to my eyes, and say, "Where is he? And what the *hell* is he?" But I restrained myself.

Alf scurried to the stern to get three long poles with boat hooks. Aage went to the seal carcass, cut off three large chunks of fat and worked them onto the boat hooks Alf brought him.

I was confused now. I couldn't see anything in the water, and wondered if somehow a killer whale was being tempted to come in close to the *Havella*, and knew that would be a dangerous sport, fooling around with anything that bloodthirsty.

Then, less than a mile out, I saw it, a V-shaped bow wave, and it was worth all of the mystery and the puzzled waiting. It came into view slowly, in segments, like film in developing fluid. As he came closer, his black nose was above water, back legs trailed like a rudder. He was moving as gracefully as a seal. These waters, dark green, hard and opaque as onyx, not clear like those of the Mediterranean or Caribbean, made it difficult to see how big he was until he got quite close. It was a polar bear, his raised head was a sun-yellowed ivory.

Hair pressed skin-smooth by the pressure of the water, he looked like a huge white fish, so skillfully did he come, front paws cleaving the water without splashing, speed about six miles an hour.

Alf immediately began filling me in on *isbjørn*, the most important animal in the north. The ice bear's greatest asset was his sense of smell. He had scented our barbecued seal blubber perhaps from as far as four or five miles. Hunters sometimes used this superb sense to kill the bear. Some thought the white animal could scent burning seal blubber from twenty miles. The hunters burned the blubber, tied a rope with a bell to another uncooked piece, then placed it in a conspicuous place close to their cabin. When the bear appeared and began eating and tinkled the bell, the hunter put his rifle through an aperture in the cabin and shot him.

As this ice bear swam toward us Alf said, with pride, as if talking about his dog that had won all of the ribbons at a show, that the animal could make fifteen-foot plunges while swimming, dive like a seal, and swim fast underwater. Air spaces in his fur, oil glands in his skin, and a thick layer of fat make him so buoyant that he can lie motionless on the surface of the water.

As the bear reached the floe, Alf stopped talking. Like a fat old man hoisting himself onto a raft, the bear put his paws on the edge of the thick floe and hauled himself onto the ice. Ten feet long, weighing about one thousand pounds, Alf estimated in a whisper.

The bear didn't make a sound. His dark eyes were without expression, the head long, tapered, snaky; water ran off the coarse white hair. As he moved closer to us on the floe, his feet made whispers of sound in the snow. Only his yellowish head and black nose stood out clearly. His weight sent the floe deeper into the water as he came toward the edge, lifted his head, and stared up at us. The frightening thing was that lack of expression, but also the direct stare, as if he was considering us some species of seal whose blubber he had scented from shore. He didn't seem the least agitated, didn't hurry his movements. This first wild polar bear I had seen chilled me. I had no idea they were so large; this one seemed to own the sea, the ice floe, and was about to take out a lease on the *Havella*. Haakon Godtliebsen's entertainment was a spine-stiffening success.

Our anchor hook was embedded in floe ice, its manila rope trailing back to the *Havella*. In one quick movement, proving strength and intelligence, using paws like hands, the bear grabbed the rope and pulled the floe closer to the boat.

As he padded to the edge near us, Alf reached a long boat hook baited with blubber toward the bear. He stood upright, easily swiping it off. I held a boat hook toward him, and he clawed the fat into his mouth so skillfully that I didn't even feel a tremor in the long pole.

Standing and swiping, he ate that seal's blubber in less than a half hour. The captain said that the bear had a hyped-up digestive system that in several hours converted an entire seal into one quart of green bile.

When we stopped feeding the bear he went down on all fours and began to act as nervous as a fox in a cage, rushing to the far end of the floe, then back. When he reached the far edge the second time, Alf and Harald quickly dragged in the anchor. Haakon had the engine purring; we pulled away, Alf and Harald coiling the anchor rope.

As I looked back at the bear agitatedly pacing the floe, Alf told me that once they had made the mistake of not moving off in time and the bear had leaped onto deck. They had had to shoot him.

11

The *Havella* carried a fourteen-foot boat, the *Jolle*, "the little boat," on her larboard side. Besides being used for viewing musk oxen, it took the crew exploring the shoreline, cruising the fjords, fishing in quiet coves or bays, and, as I would soon discover, it provided the means for obtaining a unique dinner, and for placing me in the most dangerous situation I had yet encountered.

Gray, trimmed with black, it had a deep draft, carried two pairs of oars, could comfortably seat four, six if necessary. It seemed a seaworthy little craft, but with typical Norwegian frugality it had the smallest motor I've ever seen, a two-horsepower if there is such a thing. It moved through the water well, but at a pace that made you want to take up the oars and hurry it along. I wondered what would happen if we needed an extra burst of speed in an emergency. I was to find out.

It happened near a small island that we were skirting. A flock of birds went up near shore and flew up a fjord. They winged away with the swift strokes of wildfowl, ducks. But these alternated the wing beats with periods of gliding. "Eiders," said Olsen. "They're going into Bockfjorden."

"Eiders?" I said. "Arctic ducks. I've never seen one—"

"That means you also have never eaten one," Olsen said. "I think we ought to improve your education."

"Good," I said. "How?"

"Get the *Jolle* and a shotgun and go up Bockfjorden."

He went below and came up with a shotgun, stuffing shells in his pocket. "Captain says fine. But make sure we come back with dinner."

The water was calm and the *Jolle* rode it deeply. Olsen gave a fill-in on the eider as we headed toward the fjord. They breed from the Farne Islands to Svalbard. During that breeding season, which was now past, the male has a dark stomach and a white back, the only duck that has, Olsen said. But now the sexes looked alike, dark, reddish brown, barred with black. It is the largest duck, twenty-three inches long, a fast flyer and a good diver.

We went into the fjord, the motor putt-putting, the water blue-green, the red cliffs rising almost straight up, walling us in like a moat. Suddenly it became silent; there was no sound from the sea. The cliffs were reflected in the water, the jagged shapes red and startling before us. This water that came in from the sea gave an instant sense of isolation, made you feel like an intruder.

The fjord ran inland straight as a man-made canal. The eiders were rafted about two hundred yards ahead. Olsen's scheme was to go slowly, then suddenly put on all the speed he could. These ducks had never been bothered by hunters so they would dive at the last moment, swim underwater a distance, surface, and if we were still there they would flare into the sky. The high cliffs would prevent them from flying either right or left; so they would spurt straight ahead, and, Olsen hoped, give him two shots, maybe three. We wanted just three ducks; the dinner treat would be a half an eider apiece, as only Aage could prepare them. Fjord shooting was good, Olsen said. The ducks could of course fly over the cliffs on either side, but usually they took the easiest route, straight ahead, giving the gunner a chance to get them into the air again within shooting range.

Olsen had an old side-by-side 12-gauge shotgun, a Swedish make with double triggers. He would have to be awfully fast, shoot twice, reload, and shoot again. The shot was light, and I wasn't sure it would down an eider. He said it would if you were dead on and didn't just wing a bird.

As the *Jolle* went along you knew the sea was behind you but the fjord locked it out. I looked back, caught a far gleam of water capping, then swung around just as the action began.

Olsen's scenario was word perfect. The eiders sat on the water ahead of us, their heads swiveling as the *Jolle* came at them as fast as its little motor could putt-putt. Suddenly the ducks vanished, as if something had reached up and yanked them under.

Olsen kept the *Jolle* rushing ahead. The eiders indeed were powerful swimmers. They surfaced twenty-five yards ahead of us, hesitated for a moment, then surged into the air, their wings beating and whistling.

Olsen stood up, swinging the gun with their flight, firing twice. Two ducks plummeted. He quickly reloaded, swung again with the flight of birds, wing-tipping one that left the flock of about thirty and went off like a lobbed ball.

I took the *Jolle* after it without instruction from Olsen. He slammed in another shell, stood up and fired twice at the wounded eider. It plopped into the water. I went after it first.

We had no trouble retrieving the three ducks. I hefted them as Olsen placed them in the boat. They were heavy, the brown and black feathers richly colored, glossy.

Olsen looked happy and said something I thought that I would never hear from a Norwegian. He smiled at me. "Good. I'm getting a little tired of fish."

That fjord was tempting, it tugged at you, making you want to follow it inland, back where the big glaciers waited. But Olsen had taken over and he swung the *Jolle* around and we went back toward the sea, the little motor sounding like an electric shaver.

As we entered the sea Olsen dodged a berg that came spinning along in the swell making better time than we were. It looked as blue as a cornflower as it went sailing past. The sun seemed to get trapped in that freshwater ice, giving it a color that flamed.

The *Havella* wasn't where we had left her.

Seeing that empty ocean where we expected to see the ketch made us both anxious. We looked at each other, then began searching the sea. There she was, probably four miles in the other direction. Staying to the shoreline, going slowly to avoid floating fragments of ice, Olsen pushed the little motor to its limit, with the result that I thought that we could have walked faster.

He spoke over his shoulder. "See the gulls. Kittiwakes, I think."

He stopped, cutting the motor just short of a stall. "I wish we'd brought glasses. See that lump on the shore. It's a polar bear kill. A seal. It's suspicious that the birds don't land. They're too cautious. I'm betting the bear's still around."

We sat, trying what skilled watchers do, to project ourselves out there where the bear might be. But we saw nothing except the dull brown terrain of the shoreline, rock and ice beyond, and strips of grainy snow.

The gulls still didn't swoop down on the seal, and we sat for ten minutes hoping to see the bear, then started again, Olsen taking the *Jolle* out to sea on a beeline for the *Havella*.

We were about three hundred yards from shore when he saw it.

"Something swimming this way," he said, revving the motor.

Whatever was in the water was coming fast, but I couldn't identify it.

But Alf Olsen could. "It's the bear," he said soberly. "Swimming fast."

I saw the V-wave then, the same that the bear had made when it came out to the *Havella* to investigate the burning seal blubber.

The *Havella* seemed a long way out there and suddenly I thought of the word used in fishing fleets for the big ship from which smaller boats work, "mother ship," and I knew what they meant.

I doubt that we were making three miles an hour in the *Jolle*. Behind us the bear was doing nearly twice that. Coming directly for us.

I shouldn't have done it, but sometimes curiosity is stronger than fear. I turned to watch him.

He seemed even larger than the one we had tempted to the boat with blubber. He was about one hundred yards behind us, but the sun was on him, the water was calm, and I could see him clearly. His hide was more yellow from the summer sun than the other one's had been, his ears were tight against his head, his hind legs trailed like a rudder, his front paws were oaring the water, and he was stretched straight out like an Olympic contestant in the home stretch. Even from that distance he seemed almost as large as the *Jolle*.

Alf Olsen was upset. He was the veteran; he saw the danger. So did I but it didn't help to have it spelled out so clearly. "I have seen one bear upset a sealing boat bigger than this," Olsen said slowly.

As Haakon Godtliebsen and Alf had told Fred Baldwin back in King's Bay, polar bears rarely flee from anything. When they see movement, they come straight for it. Movement can be food. Nothing, other than a killer whale or a giant walrus, is strong enough or large enough to do battle with them. And polar bears are unpredictable; you never know what they are going to do.

I thought of how we must have looked to this bear in this forsaken area where it is doubtful if he had seen humans in a boat before. The two heads sticking above the boat that wasn't much larger than he was must have puzzled him, for he suddenly stopped his forward movement. He remained stationary, paddling lazily to stay afloat, raising his snaky head out of the water to look us over, giving us a little time to make more headway. Not much. Then he started for us again.

"What do we do?" I said shakily.

"I don't know," Olsen said. "The shotgun wouldn't stop him. We could try to blind him. But if that didn't work he'd be on us in seconds."

"Do you suppose it would stop him long enough for us to get away if I kept tossing the eider ducks back to him?"

Olsen hesitated. "He might decide to come right to the source where the ducks were coming from. I just don't know."

At this point the *Jolle*'s motor sounded like it was running on wound rubber bands. Unless they were watching through binoculars the crew on the *Havella* would be unaware of our predicament. This was how tragedies often occur. Unforeseen incidents, freak happenings. A bear guarding his seal kill on a barren beach sees a boat, swims to investigate.

I knew that even in summer that water was icy, and I doubted that I could swim very long or very far if the bear did overturn the *Jolle*. And if he did spill us into the sea wouldn't a man splashing around look like a seal to him? If only you had the ability to turn off the mind during times of danger, so that you sat cold and calculating and calm. I tried it and wondered what would happen if we fired a few rounds in the water around him. Not trying to wound him, but just to discourage him. It could do a number of things, agitate him, startle him, anger him—

I almost wondered aloud, if he did approach, could we fend him off with an oar, shoot him with the shotgun, then club him? Such is the will to survive that I even considered asking Olsen if we might outmaneuver the bear by unexpectedly heading for shore and entering the fjord again. To what purpose?

The bear was back there now about seventy yards and coming fast. I was about to suggest to Olsen that we try shooting pellets around him to drive him away, when the polar bear began a curious action.

He backpaddled. Then, in an astonishing burst of speed, he swam in a big circle around us, proving that he could have run us down with ease. Breaking his circle, swinging abruptly around, he started back for shore and what was left of his seal.

I now knew exactly what arctic explorer Vilhjalmur Stefansson meant when he said, after being stalked by a polar bear, "An adventure is interesting enough in retrospect, especially to the person who didn't have it. At the time it happens it usually constitutes an extremely disagreeable experience."

I don't know what condition Olsen was in but I was trembling as I sat watching that bear swim back toward shore.

The single amusing aspect of this drama was the gulls. When they saw the bear stalking us, they lost their caution and darted down on the remains of the seal. Now, as we sat, silent and aware of what could have happened, we saw the bear burst out of the water and the birds flare into the sky.

One didn't make it. The bear, standing upright, batted it to the ground in a single, remarkably swift blow. We would have been as helpless as fish in a net in the water with that ice bear.

When we returned to the *Havella* there were no lighthearted quips about our dilemma. The big white bear was taken very seriously by the entire crew. He was smart, he was unpredictable, he was enormously strong, and he was dangerous, on record as having killed men. The combined knowledge of the five Norwegians added up to an impressive amount of information on the polar bear.

Hansen thought they were the most intelligent animals in the north. He told me of watching a seal lying near its breathing hole on an enormous ice floe, when he saw a bear three hundred yards away making an approach. There were several small floes between them, and every time the bear had to cross an open space he swam underwater. When he reached the large floe he climbed up on the ice-foot, cautiously, inch by inch, raising his head to see if the seal was still there. Suddenly, without a backward look, he slid off the ice into the water and vanished. The next action Hansen saw was the bear's head and shoulders appearing out of the breathing hole beside the seal.

"As you know, seals usually sun beside holes just large enough to admit themselves," Hansen said. "It is their life insurance. This one made a fatal mistake. That bear was so smart he judged the size of the hole before he made his move."

The white bear also knows that the seal's blowhole is only large enough to admit one seal at a time. So when he sees three or four sunning near a hole, he abandons customary caution and races in, knowing that he will get at least one as they all rush to the hole to escape.

Hansen claimed that this timing, patience, and judgment is taught polar bear cubs by their mothers, among the most devoted of animal parents. Mating in midsummer at the age of five, the female digs her lair for the January birth of one or two cubs in pressure ice hummocks or deep snow. Surprisingly, offspring from an eight-hundred-pound bear can weigh as little as two pounds. Soon the entrance to the nursery is blocked with snow and the temperature rises, as it does in an Eskimo igloo. The female remains in her den until late March or early April, in a state of semi-hibernation, living off her fat, nursing her young throughout the winter.

She keeps them with her for two years, not mating again during this period, patiently teaching them the hunting arts. Haakon Godtliebsen watched a female stalk a seal, two cubs sitting quietly observing the technique, their mother doing everything slowly, exaggerating movement so the cubs would understand the lesson.

All of the crew had seen female bears swimming in the sea with cub or cubs, following, then finally scrambling up on her back to finish the swim.

Olsen remembered one afternoon when he was sealing seeing an old she-bear and two half-grown cubs swimming in open water almost two hundred miles north of Greenland. They were heading farther north for the ice pack, which was at least another hundred miles away.

"Last year I saw an old male yellow as the nicotine stains on Sigurd's fingers," the captain said. "Must've weighed fifteen hundred pounds. He was over one hundred miles out in the open sea."

The Norwegians believed that their ice bear was becoming more of a marine than a land mammal, spending so much time in the water that it now swam almost as well as a seal or a penguin, without using back legs. "We never come out here that we don't see them in the sea," Sigurd Dal said, looking at me with a glint of humor in his eyes.

I didn't respond. I had seen my own bear in the sea. There had been nothing humorous about it.

Dal began talking about the bear's physical characteristics. Legs are jointed so they can swing in a wide circle, an aid in swimming and maneuverability. He has special arctic sunglasses, a nictitant membrane which protects his eyes from ice glare and prevents snow blindness. Toes are partially webbed, and he is the only bear with hair on the bottoms of his feet, converting them into a combination of snowshoes and paddles. Unretractable claws, kept sharp by the constant walking on ice, are precision instruments for hooking seals out of their breathing holes.

With his elongated body, tapered head, slender limbs, long neck, short ears, creamy white coat, weighing up to fifteen hundred pounds, the ice bear not only is among the largest of all predators, but is unlike any other animal. He looks like an offspring of the Ice Age, which he is, having evolved from the European brown bear during the period when glaciers moved into Eurasia and even into the northern United States. The ice bear is a single species, having developed a singular personality and physique in its northern environment. But scientists have proved its close blood relationship with brown and grizzly bears by interbreeding them in captivity, where they produced fertile young. Although extraordinarily graceful, the ice bear's rump, rising higher than his shoulders, makes him look awkward in movement. He hisses like a cat when annoyed, roars when angry or wounded, but usually is silent. It was this silence plus his aplomb that made him so frightening for me.

Hansen swore that this half-ton animal is so skillful in its element that it can walk over ice that no man can cross. He told of one coming up to within fifty yards of him over thin ice. "I stood right there looking in his direction but I didn't see him until he was that close. I wouldn't have seen him on that ice and snow at all if it wasn't for his black nose."

Olsen had heard one trapper telling of watching two bears sit down on ice near the sea. Like old gentlemen protecting their noses from the cold, they covered those black noses that betrayed them, and sat patiently waiting. Soon a bearded seal popped out of the water.

Against that snowy backdrop, perfectly camouflaged, their noses covered, the seal didn't see the bears. Quickly, one bear threw out a paw and flipped the five-hundred-pound seal out on the ice, where both pounced on it.

Several times the crew had observed another example of the clever bear covering his black nose in order to get a meal. Anchored in a fjord, they watched a bear approach a flock of eider ducks resting on the surface. The bear swam slowly, carefully, with scarcely a ripple, his nose hidden in the water, only the top of his head visible, moving like a piece of floating ice.

Suddenly the bear was among the ducks. They dove. So did he. Finally, in what seemed to the crew like ten minutes, the bear came surging to the top, an eider flapping in his mouth. These birds, alert, as I knew from my duck-hunting experience with Olsen, didn't realize that there was a polar bear around until he popped up in their midst.

The crew told me that their ice bear sometimes also provided amusement. Just last year they had seen a large male swim up to an ice floe where a ringed seal was sunning itself. This was an impatient bear. He leaped on the ice and took a hasty swipe at the seal as it escaped into the water. The bear then stood upright on the floe, picked up pieces of ice and hurled them in rage. Then he flopped down, sulking.

One early spring the captain had seen a full-grown bear sitting in the snow of a narrow fjord trying to catch low-flying snow buntings with his front paws. As the birds dodged by, he clapped his paws together, and then slowly opened them to find them empty.

Last spring the *Havella* hove to off an ice-covered island to watch four polar bears moving along the shoreline. They shambled aimlessly for a while; then one went up a small icy knoll, turned around, sat down and slid to the bottom like a child on a playground slide. Two others watched, then repeated the performance.

But the polar bear is neither clown nor villain. He is a dedicated hunter, killing only for food, or what he thinks is food. In the harsh winter of his barren land anything that moves is fair game. Living on sea ice that covers 17 percent of the globe's surface, the bear follows the sun. During the fall he comes southward; in the spring he starts north again, staying on the ice belt along the arctic coast, where seals are plentiful. His migrations (and he is constantly on the move, often traveling seventy-five miles a day) are influenced by food and ice movement. Some naturalists believe that his travels are circumpolar, from Franz Josef Land and Svalbard south along Greenland, west and north through the Canadian Arctic Archipelago, through the Beaufort Sea north of Alaska and along the northern edge of Siberia back to Svalbard.

Although most white bears spend their entire lives on moving ice, never seeing a blade of grass, there are exceptions. One was seen northeast of Great Slave Lake, seventy-five miles from the nearest sea. Another made his way up the MacKenzie River to Fort MacPherson, one hundred and fifty miles from salt water. Riding floes from the Labrador coast to Newfoundland, several have passed through the Strait of Belle Isle, between Newfoundland and Quebec, one hundred miles up the Saguenay River from the gulf.

But while they are in their normal, isolated arctic world, the chain of life there is linked to tiny, shrimplike sea organisms, "krill," that swarm in waters of low salinity. Krill swim to areas where icebergs are melting, diluting sea water. Here they feed on nutrients from the melted fresh water, the fish feed on krill, seals eat fish, and bears hunt seals.

The polar bear likes to prowl near the lightly frozen cracks in the ice. Formed by storms, tidal currents break two-foot cracks running for miles in even the heaviest ice. These tide-cracks freeze quickly, are soon covered with snow which slows freezing. Seals use these areas as breathing spots, finding it easy to pop their heads up through the new ice. When the seal surfaces for air, the waiting bear, almost always using his left paw, flips it out on the ice and kills it with one bite.

If there aren't tidal cracks, seals lie beside the breathing holes that they have kept open during the winter. Their routine of sunbathing for three minutes, then lifting their heads and looking for danger for about fifteen seconds, often is their downfall. The polar bear's timing, learned from cub days, is superb. When he sees a seal, he makes his approach slowly; using chest and front legs as runners, he slides forward on the ice almost like a sled, moving only when the seal drops its head.

Through glasses Hansen had watched one take a ringed seal in this manner. Although the distance couldn't have been more than a hundred yards, it took the patient bear almost thirty-five minutes to finally spring up and grab the unsuspecting seal.

The only creature (other than the killer whale, known to catch a bear in the water) that the polar bear fears is the walrus. Three times the bear's size, it has long, sharp tusks, a hide that is almost impossible to penetrate and can outswim and drown the bear. But the walrus is stupid and the bear is not. The captain knew the master of a sealing vessel who had talked with Eskimos who had seen a polar bear creep up on a sleeping walrus and kill it by bashing its head with a block of ice.

On a ketch sailing the Arctic Ocean, talking about wild polar bears with Norwegians who know the animals from their own observations, and from conversations with seamen, sealers, trappers, and hunters, was, for me, akin to being the first to debrief spacemen when they return from the moon.

It is especially impressive when you have seen the subject of their conversations so close that you note the scars on ears and the expression, or fearful lack of it, in their dark, staring eyes.

And it is a conversation with unequaled drama, for you never know when you are going to look over your shoulder at the sea and see the object under discussion swimming by.

12

The *Havella* had become not only a dominant personality but a drug. Her rolling motion soothed me; she had cut me adrift. The other me that I had left behind on land had diminished to the point where I saw mostly shadows and some brief flashes of unreal scenes of someone else's life. I lived in the world of the crew, the time of today, wasting no thought on yesterday or tomorrow. It was a habit of happiness that I hoped I could keep. I was addicted to those hours when I stood with my hands on the wheel, before me the vastness of the ocean with no sign of human life, the *Havella* gliding through the water tossing back foam on either side of her bow, that insolent sun making the day dazzling, erasing the clouds, turning the water a calm, benevolent green.

This was the sea at peace with itself, reminding me of a great cat purring, not showing the strength beneath its spotted hide, but all the time I knew it was there, the fierce leap and the roar, the terrible talons retracted, like the waves that live in the water without breaking. I wrapped my fingers around the wheel for the self-deluding pleasure of feeling in control, but I didn't have to steer, the *Havella* skimmed along like she was half gull, half dolphin, in her element, where only a touch of the finger was needed to guide her. Sounds were muted; the prow produced a pleasant soft sizzle as it cut through the water, which fell back lapping the hull, sighing as it rose, moaning as the hull fell back into the trough of the sea. It was hypnotic.

This might be a hard, stark land, almost impossible to live in during the winter, but now, in summer, it was a world of diamond beauty, the iced islands catching the constant sun in a gem reflection, throwing it back in a spectrum of colors ranging from deep mauve to palest pink. It was a world of uncluttered sea, rare birds, unique isolation, of a silence that sang a siren song. It also was a world of waiting glaciers, which I was anxious to see up close.

Now I heard the captain clumping up from below. He came into the wheelhouse in his hitching, peg-leg stride, looking at me with blue eyes that were as steady as a gun barrel.

"Keep an eye open for an island coming up before long," he said. "There may be something on it I want you to see."

The captain was openly proud of Svalbard and liked to surprise me with new sights, like opening a box of treasures and dangling a rare gem before my eyes. From the very first, with that view of the musk oxen, and the bits and pieces of knowledge he had on everything from seals and polar bears to the habits of the sea birds, he had impressed me with his educated enthusiasm.

It is uncommon to come across a man who not only loves but knows his country the way Haakon Godtliebsen did. I remembered well a guide taking me through some wild Adirondack Mountain terrain who couldn't identify most trees or plants, and knew little about the wildlife there except the dates the hunting season opened on them and what the bag limits were. And that wasn't unusual. Most men take their world for granted.

Not the captain. He seemed as excited and as interested as I was each time we saw a bird or a seal, or even the sun glinting in a spectacular way on a chunk of floating ice. He had even played the game with me of giving drifting ice identities, and had more imagination than I at it. He saw one small iceberg poking just a blue tip above water, twisting and turning in the current, as a young killer whale just out of the womb.

Right now the sun dazzle on the water made it difficult to look steadily for any length of time. But I had learned days ago if I was the pilot then I was the pilot. You had the wheel, you steered the ship. There wasn't any fog right now and I hoped that there wouldn't be any.

After that traumatic encounter with the looming mirage, the captain, in his clear, concise way, had also explained what caused the fog that was swirling around it and the banks of it that mysteriously appeared over the Arctic Ocean before us as if someone had dropped a smoke bomb. It is simply cloud at lower level, Haakon told me. Fog is made up of tiny water droplets which are suspended in the air. This condensation is produced by warm air gusting across a cold land or sea surface, or the mixing of warm and cold airstreams. Both situations occurred here.

I was frank with myself. When I was at the wheel fog frightened me. Not just because a looming mirage might pop out of a fog bank, but because it made you instantly blind, lost in what seemed like all-enveloping liquid wool. In fact, the captain told me that this arctic fog reduced visibility to less than one kilometer. And I remembered that that was six-tenths of a mile.

Now in the clear sunlight coming up off the starboard side ahead was just the faintest indication that there was something on the horizon. The sea was smooth, then it abruptly scalloped just above the curvature of the earth which restricts vision eight inches to the mile. Another mile out and I wouldn't have seen the cold chalk scallop that marked the island edge.

As the view came up, suddenly off our bow was a splatter of black guillemots. The little white-breasted auks burst up in a dribble against the sky, in an untidy line like the too-swift stroke of an artist, the paint running off in odd little birdlike blobs.

I hadn't startled them as they dozed on the warm sunlit sea. Why had they suddenly taken off fifty yards from our bow? Normally these were peaceful birds that floated buoyantly on the ocean and watched us go by.

A suddenly breaking V wave centering where the birds had leaped into the air was the answer. I cut my speed and went off course to come up alongside it.

As I drew near, the polar bear lifted his head in a menacing gesture, his cold black eyes defiant. I looked down on him, his front paws cleaving the water as cleanly as racing oars, his ten-foot body looking twice its size in the distorting, gray-green water. His head was a faded yellow, and half of one ear was missing.

Staying abreast of the bear, I suddenly had a silly thought as he pulled his head back and stretched straight out, swimming faster, trying to outdistance me. Retribution. Giving in to the childish impulse, I wheeled the *Havella* in a wide turn and took her in a slow circle around the bear.

But I got no satisfaction out of it, for the bear, keeping up his steady, powerful stroke, back legs trailing, looking like a long, hairy fish, ignored me, and headed straight out to sea.

So I straightened the *Havella* and took her toward that scalloped edge of distant shore. A scuffing noise made me swing around.

The entire crew stood there, grinning. I hadn't heard them come from below.

"I guess you showed him," Olsen said, making me feel nine years old, caught with my hand in my visiting aunt's purse.

"Let me take her now," Haakon said, still grinning. "I want

you to watch the shore with binoculars. Maybe you won't see anything. Maybe you will. They're usually on this island."

He handed me the glasses and with a feeling of frustration, I watched him take over the *Havella*. I'd never be able to handle her with that ease, that superb confidence. The wheel seemed an extension of him, whereas I hung onto it like some strange growth.

It was a calm day. Waves capped white in the distance, but they were gentle by the time they reached us. There was a mild offshore breeze, just enough to fluff the feathers on the glaucous gulls as they sat down on the water to our larboard side. Ice floes sailed by as serenely as swans and the *Havella* went like the gull-dolphin that she was toward shore.

Olsen came and stood beside me at the rail. "Kvitøya is the island," he said. "Inland it's mostly covered with ice but it is always clear on shore this time of year. We can't get too close though. Too rocky and shallow inshore. We could go in a ways with the *Jolle,* but what's the point? You'll be able to see what the captain has in mind from deck. Besides, we're not going to spend much time here. We've got some pushing ahead."

I asked what he meant by pushing, and wondered what it was the captain wanted me to see.

"Both questions will answer themselves," he said calmly, pointing. "There's the island now. Another fifty yards in, start glassing the shoreline."

Like some of the other islands this reared up as if there was nothing there except a big ice-slicked rocky mountain.

The captain brought the *Havella* in and turned her broadside to the island. I put the binoculars on the shoreline. It was strewn with rocks and pebbles, white and clean as bones, without snow or ice, and back a few feet vegetation that looked like brown moss hugged the ground closely. I carefully glassed as much of the shoreline as I could see. In some places there were outcroppings of large jagged slabs of rock, upended and jumbled as if tossed there by a tornado. Suddenly pieces of the mosslike vegetation were in motion. I focused and found that I had picked up two furry creatures, followed by four smaller ones.

The six animals had short faces, low ears, upper portions of their bodies were deep brown, the lower a honey buff.

"Arctic foxes," Olsen said. "Male, female, and four kits. This part of the island is a favorite place for foxes. Those big rocks make good dens and they can hunt for sea birds and their eggs nearby and the fish and shellfish exposed at low tide offshore."

I had never seen an Arctic fox but had thought that they were white. Olsen said that they were white in winter, so pure a white that it blanked them out against the snowy background, giving them perfect camouflage protection.

The kits were frolicking along the beach like kittens, the adult pair sitting on their haunches watching. The young foxes ventured into the water gingerly, glancing back at their parents as if seeking guidance.

"They can swim," Olsen said, "but don't seem to like the water and go into it only in an emergency." He thought these young ones had been born in May, about fifty-two days after the mating, and would be on their own by October. "A vixen can have as many as a dozen, but the average is four to eight, each kit weighing three ounces at birth."

The adult foxes looked quite large, but Dal, who had come back from his usual position at the bow, said that was sort of an illusion. Their bodies were only twenty inches long, the flagged tails twelve inches, and they weighed anywhere from seven to fifteen pounds.

"The fur makes them look larger," Dal said. "It's so thick that only temperatures of twenty-five degrees below zero make them increase their metabolic rate. Even a bone-chilling sixty below doesn't seem to bother Arctic foxes."

None of the crew was cute or pompous with his knowledge. It came out as natural as talk about the weather. Olsen picked up on the conversation on the fur saying that it gave such protection from the cold that the fox, unlike most other animals, didn't have to increase its food intake when the temperature dropped and thus could live in areas where food was scarce.

"When I've been sealing in the winter I've seen Arctic foxes way out at sea on icebergs and floes. They often stay on the pack ice through the winter months, living on gulls and sea birds that they catch quick as a cat."

Mainly, though, in the winter they live off polar bears. Each adult bear has one or several foxes following it. When the polar bear kills a seal, eats its full, then leaves it for a while, the foxes dart in and finish the remains. It's a dangerous way to make a living, for the bear will kill the foxes if he can. But they usually are too swift, too agile.

"That's only in winter," Olsen said. "The foxes don't bother the bears in summer. There's plenty of food around then. Their favorite meal is lemmings, but they'll eat anything they can find, even dead fish."

"It's a sight to see these foxes hunting the bird cliffs," Dal broke in. "They're so skillful they can walk across the face of a sheer cliff looking for the nests of murres."

Olsen relieved the captain at the wheel, and he came over to where I was still watching the foxes through the glasses, telling me that they moult their white coats gradually beginning in February, and that he had seen white foxes with brown tails and legs.

"I think we go now," the captain said abruptly. "I wanted you to see these clever animals. They are not in many places anymore. Their thick white fur is too popular with the ladies. They've been shot and trapped out pretty much. Except up here where there still may be more foxes than men."

Dal held up a big hand with his fingers crossed. "Hope it holds that way. Foxes are prettier than people."

Alf Olsen took the *Havella* out to sea, then straightened her, paralleling the shore, and then kept her at about an eight-knot speed.

The captain and Sigurd Dal were deep in conversation. In a few minutes Dal went below and Hansen came up and stood talking with the captain.

I knew we were only a matter of days from our destination, but had not questioned Haakon Godtliebsen about time, distance, and all of the rest of it. He was a man who did things his own way and when he was ready to fill me in he would do so. Also every aspect of this world was new to me, from musk oxen to Arctic foxes, and the captain saw to it that my hours were occupied. When he thought that I might be restless he suggested that I take over the wheel.

Actually it was impossible to be restless through boredom. Every sense seemed sandpapered to a fine point. Smells were recognized and identified by a nose that seemed not to be my own. Aage Rutwold's meals came wafting up from the galley as if they each had a name written on the wind, a beef pot roast with red cabbage, a fish stew with tomato, pork scallops in butter and white wine. I read our menu with my nose. My hearing amazed me. Over the smooth beat of the *Havella*'s motor I could now hear a gull come down on the water and sometimes identify it by the splash; even against the sun, through my dark glasses, I could pick up ice in the distance and was beginning to tell from quite far away whether it was floe or berg. But the soul is not a sense; it is a submerged being all by itself. I wasn't certain yet what this new freedom from fret and friction and competition had done to it. But I knew that there was something here for it that was immensely more valuable than touring France's vineyard country, or even lazing on a houseboat in Kashmir. It was not only being soothed but strengthened. It would also be tested.

I had confided to the captain that I would like to walk on a glacier, feeling somewhat childish when I admitted it, but Haakon said that he understood and had also wanted to do the same thing, and that he thought it would be possible. As usual, he excited my imagination by telling me that if we did get up on a glacier there was a creature he wanted to show me, one that actually lived in the ice of the glacier. Also, typically, he would not go into detail, and I knew better than to prod him and turn the whole thing into an anticlimax.

As I watched the captain in what was obviously a conference, first with Dal, now with Hansen, my mind went to the gray-green water beneath us and I walked to the rail and stared down, turning over in my mind the little I knew about this still mysterious ocean lying at the edge of the North Pole. The Arctic Ocean included, with the Norwegian and Greenland seas, and the Barents Sea, which is actually a gulf of the Greenland sea, about 5,400,000 square miles. A unique feature was its wide continental shelf supporting groups of islands—Svalbard, Greenland, Franz Josef Land, Novaya Zemlya, and the Canadian Arctic islands.

I also was aware that this was a frighteningly deep ocean, that depths of 17,880 feet had been reached, and that in 1949 the Russians had discovered a great mountain range in the Arctic Ocean at a depth of 12,000 feet. It extends for many miles, dividing the ocean into an eastern and western basin. Named the Lomonosov Range, in some places the submerged mountains rise to within 3,000 feet of the surface.

This also was an ocean two-thirds of which was covered by drifting pack ice. I vaguely knew that the circulation, the currents twisting beneath me, constituted a complex movement dependent upon winds, temperature, salinity, and the rotation of the earth. I dimly remembered also that some of the surface currents in this polar sea had a series of subsurface currents and that the ocean maintained a balance in temperature with these currents. Some scientists also believed that those subsurface currents were responsible for the distribution of heat over much of the world. That was it, my sum knowledge of the ocean we were riding like a man on horseback.

Right now to the larboard side I saw a large patch of vivid emerald green, looking as if someone had just dumped a pail of paint overboard. The captain had told me that this was caused by diatoms, a type of one-cell algae created in warm deep layers of water, providing food for pelagic plants.

Our calm day was beginning to come apart. The water was capping directly ahead of us, a brisk, hat-snatching wind had sprung up, and coming from the direction of the island where we had seen the Arctic foxes was a spectacular formation of clouds pushing toward us like the prows of giant white ghost ships. I had seen them twice before in mountainous areas. Called wave clouds because air rides up in waves as it passes over mountains, these wave crests condense water vapor, forming clouds of great smooth shapes. They were sailing across the sky like an armada that was going to run us down.

In the wheelhouse Haakon, Hansen, and Dal were leaning over a chart and Alf was at the wheel. Finally, the captain took the wheel from Alf. Hansen went below, Dal forward, and Alf Olsen came over to join me at the rail, face sober. Aage Rutwold hurried from below and was having an animated conversation with the captain.

"When he's finished talking with Aage the captain wants to see you," Olsen said.

"What's the matter?"

"Nothing serious," Olsen said. "The captain will tell you."

Aage came out and immediately went below. The captain beckoned me from the wheel.

As I entered the wheelhouse his calm blue eyes pulled me in like a net.

"Did you get very sick on the old girl, the *Lyngen*?" he asked me gently.

"Some," I said, puzzled. "But everybody did. She was a tub, not a bird like the *Havella*."

His eyes left my face and stared through the wheelhouse window. "We will be getting some heavy seas soon. When it happens I don't want you to leave the wheelhouse." His eyes swung back to me. "You know about the Gulf Stream?"

"A little. Alf told me some. I've read some."

He smiled. "Alf. Yes. We know about the Gulf Stream up here. It pushes back the ice in this ocean so we can navigate it. It gives us better weather—" He hesitated. "It will also give us bad water for a while."

"I'm not worried," I said quickly. "Sigurd is the ice pilot, you're the bad-water pilot."

He gave me that familiar tolerant half-smile that made me feel like a comedian who was trying too hard.

His smile went. "The Gulf Stream's eighty-five million tons of water a second splits at forty-five degrees north. One current then swings south along the Spanish peninsula and the northwest coast of Africa and becomes the cool Canaries current. The other split in the Gulf Stream goes northeast, passing the western coasts of the British Isles and Scandinavia as a warm current, the North Atlantic Drift. It then enters here, the Arctic Ocean. As the warm surface water of the North Atlantic Drift enters, the Arctic Ocean releases cold water. Some of that water then goes south, swings past the northeast coast of North America as the Labrador Current."

He left me then for a moment, eyes on the wheel in his hands. "No one knows why," he said finally, "but where those two currents, the North Atlantic Drift and the cold water spurted out by the Arctic Ocean, meet you might say the seas go a little crazy."

He had finally gotten to me. His personality was calm, low key. If he said the seas go a little crazy it had to be an understatement.

I went back on deck and stood at the rail watching that armada of wave clouds move overhead, saw the wind kicking up waves. For the next hour it was choppy, but nothing to get alarmed about.

Then I heard a roar and looked ahead. Probably a mile straight in front of us the seas churned in a boiling mountain of foam. The wind had swung behind us, pushing us forward at a frightening rate.

Dal came rushing from the bow. "Go in the wheelhouse," he said. He went below and came up with Hansen and Rutwold. Olsen was already beside the captain, the six of us shoulder to shoulder in the wheelhouse.

Then it was as the captain had said. The seas went a little crazy.

The waves rushing at us were at least twenty feet high lashing across the deck, washing astern. The *Havella* began pitch-poling, the alternate steep rise of her bow and stern making me grit my teeth to hold down the nausea.

It seemed impossible that any sea could treat the *Havella* this way, make her react in a manner other than her smooth, controlled glide. I saw that the captain had thrust his belly and chest against the wheel as the *Havella* went into a steep roll to starboard.

As the waves hurled against us she staggered, then rose on a crest and seemed to founder, going into an abrupt angle of thirty degrees of roll.

I could see nothing around us now but spumes, then great gushing fountains of white water, smashing against the wheelhouse window.

The waves were hitting from all angles, hard water that seemed to be battering a coral reef against our sides. We were rocked with every wave blow, the *Havella* shuddering like a stricken animal. She would rise on a wave crest, climbing up on the gray-green hill of rushing water, pushing her nose through it, then falling down on the other side, flooding her foredeck with water that rushed forward like a mass of angry hissing serpents.

Aage Rutwold tapped my shoulder and handed me a pail. I showed my gratitude with my eyes, then my stomach, as I retched into the pail.

On the port beam a clifflike wave hit us a blow that almost flipped the *Havella* over. But somehow the captain swung her around.

Now she was plunging bow first, then rolling starboard thirty degrees, very nearly on her side, as she corkscrewed into the sea.

We were like flies on a ceiling, hanging onto stanchions. Waves would hurl at us one after the other, never letting up; the *Havella*'s bow would rise up on a giant wave, seem to slice it in two, the halves thundering on deck, plowing astern.

An astute philosopher wrote, "Each hour of pleasure is paid for with an hour of pain." Violent seasickness isn't exactly pain; it's worse. It is a gut-wrenching nausea that goes like fire throughout your entire system making you feel as if your head should be amputated and your stomach replaced. I had been somewhat seasick on the *Lyngen*. She rolled like a bathtub when she hit hard water, but there were over a hundred others there to share the misery and it was not a sustained seasickness, it came and went, and I wasn't surrounded by expert seamen hardened to whatever the sea could produce who looked at you when you vomited like some specimen that had been washed up on deck. It wasn't that they weren't sympathetic; it was just that I must have developed into an object of curiosity, and they probably were interested in how much bile one man could produce.

Let me also affirm the accuracy of the encyclopedia description of seasickness that states there are great physical prostration, pallor (I even *felt* pale), cold sweats and feeble pulse, accompanied by mental depression and wretchedness. Although these symptoms were almost instant and simple to recognize, turning a man into an approximation of a barely warm corpse that was leaking its life away through its constantly open mouth, the causes of seasickness are quite complicated.

The pitching and rolling motion of the ship apparently disturbs the intricate balancing system of the semicircular canals of the inner ear. But there is more involved. Visual, mental, and olfactory impressions also contribute. No medicine has yet been discovered to effectively help this sickness. We can put men on the moon, transplant kidneys, place a machine in the chest to aid the heart, but we are helpless when the sea makes us sick. This may be the ultimate mastery of the sea over man.

We spent two days pitching and fighting through that confluence of waters. There was one small helpful lesson that I had learned from what proved to be the mild seasickness on the *Lyngen*: there were two items that the stomach would hold, at least for a while—bread and cheese. And there was also some strange sort of satisfaction when I observed that even the crew ate nothing else during those forty-eight hours.

Perhaps I make too much of this experience. But I know two things for certain. My admiration for the crew of the *Havella* doubled. They had gone through that watery hell often. Also, if I had the choice, I would never do it again. Fortunately, on the return trip we followed a different route.

13

The sea was flat. Gulls were in a ragged flight beyond us making motions like ballerinas; suddenly four rare Ross's gulls dropped out of the dim sun and skimmed low over us, the pink markings on them like fresh paint. The *Havella* was in her smooth, controlled glide again.

Peace.

I was a whole man again, the only sign that we had been attacked by the sea was the *Jolle*, still full of water. The crew had inspected the *Havella* as carefully as if she were alive, searching for cuts and bruises, and had announced that apparently, as far as they could see right now, we were in good shape, even that combined strength of the warm waters of the Gulf Stream and the cold waters of the Arctic Ocean hadn't been able to hurt the *Havella*. The crew didn't proudly say that the reason was that she had been built with Norwegian know-how and hands, but it was implicit in the way they acted after the beating she had taken.

Or perhaps it wasn't a beating at all. Maybe this was just

part of sailing the Arctic Ocean in a craft designed for it, manned by seamen who were used to it and equal to it.

"The sea she is like a spirited horse you ride," Haakon Godtliebsen had said after it was all over. "She lets you on her back but every once in a while she has to show you that she isn't your slave."

That was the final word. There was no more. It was over. The wind also had vanished. Suddenly I was ravenous.

I went down to the galley to find Aage at his little stove, stirring a pot of aromatic vegetable soup that set my appetite to raging. Without a word, he began manufacturing a sandwich of cold lamb, meat an inch and a half thick on richly buttered bread, black pepper sprinkled on, a thin spread of tart German mustard.

Eyes amused, he handed me the sandwich and a napkin. "Your stomach will thank you," he said.

"Both of us thank you," I said, wondering how it would set. Aage was right, my stomach purred like a cat. I ate half of the sandwich while I watched him boil some thread-thin noodles to go into the soup, then went up on deck to finish the lamb in the sunshine.

The gulls were still doing their wing dance on the horizon. I finished the sandwich and looked at the captain in the wheelhouse. He motioned for me to join him. Sigurd Dal was beside him going over the chart. The rest of the crew were below.

The *Havella* was going across the water gracefully as a deer crossing a meadow. It was colder now, probably about thirty-two degrees. When an occasional spray flew up from the ocean and touched my face it had the feel of ice.

"We're not far now," the captain said as I entered. "Less than seventy-five miles, I think."

Dal told me that we were navigating by degrees now on the chart, noting the position along the northeast coast of Nordaustlandet Island where the fjord we were looking for was supposed to have been released from its prison of ice. Beyond was a small bay we would enter if it was open, and beyond that was the lake that had been isolated for so long.

"Soon," Dal said, "we should be able to see Nordaustlandet. Shortly after that I think I am going to pay for my passage—"

I looked at him.

He nodded. "Yes, pretty far north here. We should see ice in the water."

"Much?" I said.

He nodded.

The captain didn't say anything.

"Few minutes you should go on deck," Dal said. "Nordaustlandet can be seen. The edge anyway."

He stood beside me at the rail while we searched in the direction he pointed, northwest. For a while I could see only waves kicking up. A flock of black guillemots appeared, a moving black line drawn across my vision, then I saw the ice-glitter of the island.

It blazed like a distant dawn coming up and seemed as immense as that morning light on the horizon.

"It's a big island," Dal said. "We'll head right for it. Then follow a lead along its coastline to the degree point on the chart."

He explained that we were heading toward shore where he was hoping we would find open water, a "lead" that we could use as a water lane along the coast. In the summer ice melts more rapidly near the coasts. Water from the land and rivers carries continuous supplies of heat into the sea, where the atmosphere also has been warmed by the nearby land, which absorbs heat during the arctic summer. The water action from below also helps break up the ice foot along the shore. This combination of conditions melts the ice, forming the open water between the ice field and the shore.

Dal stood beside me for a couple of minutes longer, then went up to the bow. I saw the captain prop open the door of the wheelhouse, then go back to the wheel, his face set in a way it hadn't been even during those two days of what he called "hard" water.

I rarely looked at my watch. What difference did it make? Now, for some reason, habit, reflex, nervousness, I saw that it was midnight.

The sun hung low in the western sky, a melting copper ball, light flowed from it like water, astonishing purple light which fell on the snow and ice of Nordaustlandet, flashing back at us a rainbow of colors, the sight making your heart rise to your throat. Directly ahead of us the water was the pale green shade of rare Chinese jade; the few scattered bergs and ice floes were reflected in the sea as if they had been etched there. The *Havella* was throwing back silver wings of water.

Someone coughed. Olsen came out of the hatchway and stood at my elbow. Minutes later Aage Rutwold joined us, then Hansen. It was almost as ominous a situation as it had been with the six of us standing shoulder to shoulder in the wheelhouse when we staggered through the smashing seas.

Sigurd Dal's words about paying for his passage made me somewhat uneasy. Every man in the crew was a master of understatement. There had been ice everywhere on this journey —the sea was afloat with it, floes, bergs, splintered flat ice, large chunks—but until now it had been easy to avoid. There was no darkness, so no danger of smashing into ice that we couldn't see. Fog was disturbing and deadly, but so far we had been lucky. There had been a short period of worry when we encountered the large wind-driven ice sculptured in interesting shapes. But that we had drifted through without trouble.

I knew that the fields of drifting ice in the arctic seas were half the size of all of North America, a vast wasteland extending from Alaska, Canada, and Greenland, across the North Pole to Siberia and here to Svalbard. And I had been told by the crew that far from being stationary, the ice in the Arctic Ocean roared with action. Near the North Pole the floes grind constantly, the force of tides and strong winds throwing up great slabs of ice as high as a church steeple. But that was pack ice, drift ice. So far we had seen little of that. Pushing farther north toward the Pole, as we were doing, it was possible, even in summer, to run into enormous fields of this ice, the ice that had trapped explorers, clutching them in its grip for years.

What kind of ice would Dal guide us through "to pay his passage"?

Right now we were encountering the usual floes that were as natural a part of the scene here as swimming pools and golf courses in Westchester County. I was beginning to take them for granted, but now I eyed the blue-green ice sailing by with a bit of foreboding and with a speculative eye. How would it be to have a hundred of those side by side? And how would it be to have an iceberg poke a deadly head out of the middle of that raft of floes, an iceberg the size of the *Havella* on the surface, the other nine-tenths hidden beneath the water?

That's the way with the mind. It will never leave well enough alone. It immediately takes thought strands and starts embroidering intricate patterns, either fantasying to make us happy or weaving disaster designs to frustrate.

My happy medium was to think about Dal out there at the bow, peering ahead, a man who gave you confidence because he obviously had confidence in himself. Over twenty years as an ice pilot. A pro. And the captain. The way he had brought us through those waters that had gone a little crazy. Another pro. So I relaxed.

Until I saw it.

It came up like that looming mirage breaking through the floating circle of fog. Only there was no deceiving fog here; no figment iceberg created by freak temperature.

Dead ahead was a huge expanse of a solid ice field, looking completely frozen in, impenetrable.

There was no doubt about it. The sun had moved up quite a ways from its midnight horizon rim and fell clearly upon it, brighter than full moonlight, not as bright as a noon sun, but it hovered over that ice field like an airfield searchlight, pointing up various features, jammed-up floes, the shark-fin points of icebergs, gray, shabby-looking ice, pieces that floated like shattered shale. It was a mess.

Not a man at the rail said a word. Sigurd Dal was in command now. This was why he had come along. It looked like he had an impossible task, sturdy rescue boat design, double hull or not.

I was thankful for one thing at the moment. I didn't think trying to get through an ice field would make me seasick.

As we neared the ice the captain throttled down, the *Havella*'s diesel pumping like a beating heart. We nudged gently into the ice field and cautiously started through, Sigurd Dal shouting back to the captain in Norwegian, the words spaced, terse.

I stood at the rail fascinated, like a man cornered, watching a poisonous snake slither in to attack. As the *Havella*'s prow parted the ice, the hidden sea broke free and ran back on either side of the ketch, green and heavy as swamp water, white shards of broken ice floating in it like feathers.

Sounds were only the soft beat of the motor, the crunching of ice, much less of a noise than I thought it would be, and the harsh words Dal kept flinging back to the captain.

Ahead I could still see the glitter of the icebound island we were making for, gulls along its shore looking like they were sewing seams in the low-hanging white clouds, and stretching in what seemed to me for many miles, the ice field.

I thought of Nansen and Amundsen, both locked in ice like this for years, and I wondered again how they had kept their equilibrium, how they had fought the boredom, the hopeless feeling, the frustration of not being able to break out of their chains of ice. They had been in the ice in winter; this was summer and the sea was running free beneath us.

It didn't seem that way now—here it was a frapped sea, a stagnant sea, that we were trudging through with a constant grinding noise and resistance as if we were scraping the bottom.

Much of the ice still had snow on it, making it deceptive, difficult to judge. Dal was doing a masterful job of guiding us through; the grinding noise, not loud, but steady, was the small ice we were riding over, bits and pieces of storm-shattered floes. We were very lucky that there wasn't any fog, for that could get even an ice pilot of Dal's talent in trouble.

The captain was being exceedingly cautious. We were moving more slowly than a man ambling along a seashore searching for shells, picking our way. It wasn't a straight line we were sailing. Haakon not only was taking directions from Dal by voice but watching ahead, working very hard at the wheel, steering starboard when told, larboard when the command came back, sometimes reversing, then taking a new direction.

With the motor running so slowly I could hear the sound of the ice in the water ahead of us and all around us, a creaking, a groaning, sometimes a splintering as we sliced through an underwater floe.

Sometimes tips of icebergs would appear off our bow and sides, glistening blue-green beneath the surface, looking like sharks basking. But these glacier calves were more dangerous to us than any shark.

The way Haakon Godtliebsen was taking his ship through the ice made me think of the patient polar bear advancing on a seal, using its body as a sled, pushing ahead slow inch by inch, timing precise, perfect.

Then I almost fell overboard.

The *Havella* reeled, fell back as if she had run into the side of a cliff, shaking all the way back to her stern, the force of the collision shaking us loose from the rail.

The captain reversed, slowly backing off from whatever he had struck.

"Iceberg," Olsen said, going into the wheelhouse to check with the captain.

I had been told that the ice of the bergs was as hard and as sharp as steel. It had sunk craft a hundred times the size of the *Havella*.

Olsen was the nimble one. The captain held the *Havella* stationary and Olsen went over the rope ladder at the bow, taking direction from Dal, and stood on a mass of jammed floes, inspecting the ketch's hull.

He came back up, grinning. "She held," he said proudly. "A pretty good dent. But we're all right."

Crazy seas. Colliding with an iceberg. What else could this ship take?

How come we had hit the berg?

Submerged, Olsen told me. Dal couldn't see it. It was hidden, not only in the water, but massed in with floes and other ice.

We had been in the ice for two hours, Olsen said, and he had checked with Dal and he thought that we would be in it perhaps two more hours. It wasn't an enormous ice field, just normal for this part of the coast for this time of the year. It seemed enormous to me. And right now, regardless of that Midnight Sun that erased time, I was looking at my watch. For the first time on this journey the minutes were hanging heavily. And like waiting for the man in the apartment over yours to drop the second shoe so you could go to sleep, I kept waiting for us to run into the rocklike side of another sneaky submerged iceberg, and thought of how these great hunks of ice had been misnamed. Calves. They were innocent, harmless creatures that frolicked in green meadows. These born of ice caps were deadly, lying in wait to smash anything that approached.

Although it was anything but a game, and certainly was in slow motion, in the exhibition of professional skill the teamwork of the captain and the ice pilot reminded me of football, Sigurd quarterbacking from the bow, shouting back signals, Haakon spinning the *Havella* through that ice like a broken field runner, never actually getting tackled, coming close with that iceberg, staggering, but shaking off the tackle, then being grabbed several times again as we bumped a big hunk of ice or sheered through a drifting sheet.

As we made our tortuous way, Alf Olsen, I am sure hoping to take my mind off running through the rest of that blockade, talked about ice. I'm not certain that was the way to do it. A game of gin rummy below, away from the sight of that frozen sea, would have been more effective. But I appreciated the effort.

This wasn't really an ice field we were trying to move through. An ice field is the largest of sea ice areas, and the ice around us wasn't that. This was an ice pack, floating ice driven closely together by wind and tide, but an ice pack also is a term used to describe the entire area of ice in the Arctic Ocean.

Although, because of our extremely slow, cautious pace, we would take probably a total of four hours to break out of this ice, Olsen considered it a small concentration, telling me that he had seen pack ice fifty times this size.

The ice we were negotiating was composed mainly of three varieties: a small amount of ice calving from glaciers; that which formed on fjords and the sea in winter and still hadn't melted; and drift ice borne in by currents and wind. The large amount of drift ice was partially broken water ice and old polar ice drifting from the north and northeast.

Olsen thought that we had hit a berg bit, which could be either a piece of glacier ice about the size of a house, or a growler, which had the same origin but was somewhat smaller. He didn't think that there was too much polar ice ahead of us—that is, thick, heavy ice more than a year old.

With the ice crunching beneath us, Olsen explained that by freezing underneath in the winter and early spring, and melting on the surface in summer, the ice lives for years. In pack ice there are ice floes of various ages, from the inch-thick ice in the open channels, to the big floes, several years old, and the ice jammed into hummocks that can rise thirty feet above the water and extend almost three hundred feet beneath the surface.

It begins to freeze when the water has cooled to about 28°F, and small crystals form, soon growing an inch in length, then increasing until the surface is covered with the soft crystals, which are known as slush ice. It sticks together like thick gooey oatmeal a foot thick, then forms lumps of varying sizes which become glued together in a rough blanket of ice. If undisturbed by wind and current the entire surface freezes solid with this new ice, which grows rapidly, reaching a thickness of five inches in two days. Then growth slows, the ice reaching a thickness of three feet in two weeks, perhaps nine feet in a year.

It takes several years for it to thicken to fifteen feet. The slow growth results from the ice itself, which is a poor conductor of heat; thus it protects the surface of the water beneath it from rapid cooling. Arctic ice is 50 percent thicker than that in the Antarctic because there is more snow in that region and snow is even less of a heat conductor than ice.

Eventually, by midwinter, the thickening ice covers the sea

in a solid sheet, which, although thick, is still somewhat controlled by wind, currents, and tide that grind it, crush it, and break it apart. With spring and stronger sun the thaw starts, the snow melts, the floes separate and float away in ice-free water that is opened by wind and currents.

"This pack ice," Olsen said, "moves about ten miles a day. Some of this probably came from the pack close to the North Pole."

We stood silently now watching the teamwork of the captain and the ice pilot.

I knew it was over when Dal came walking slowly back from the bow.

Alf Olsen motioned me to follow him to the bow. We had reached the outside edge of the ice pack. I looked back. It stretched behind us, the sea still looking like it was frozen into a solid mass. I could see signs of the trail we had made—broken ice, floes split, some gleams of water.

The captain, on his own now, brought the *Havella* up beside a flattened iceberg. Olsen threw the rope ladder over and, a hatchet and bucket in hand, went over the side and onto the berg, and began chopping ice.

Aage Rutwold came from below with a bottle of amber liquor and a tray of squat, thick glasses. We all joined the captain in the wheelhouse. Aage filled the glasses with the berg ice and poured the amber liquor over it, serving the captain first, the ice pilot second, the silence and solemnity making it ritualistic.

As the captain raised his glass, the first to drink, I saw a line of perspiration standing out like an old scar just under his hairline. It was the only visible sign of stress that he had shown since we began this journey.

As we all held our glasses high in a silent toast, then downed it, the liquid going down as if ignited, the captain told me that this was a special aquavit, which I knew without being told. Not only did it have a special authority, but the other aquavit was colorless; this was a burnt gold. Called *linje akevitt*, it had been stored in huge sherry vats of New Orleans oak and traveled in the hold of a cargo ship from Norway to Australia and back.

The captain held up his second glass and looked at it melting the ice. "It gets this special flavor from the rolling of the ship on the long voyage," he said, adding "Skoal!" and drinking it in one gulp. "And from the change in climate."

He took a handkerchief from his pocket and wiped the sweat from his forehead.

"Alf," he said. "Take her in. We'll go right for Nordaustlandet."

14

Until now I had not met a glacier face to face. They stood in the background, somber blue giants pondering our approach, the Midnight Sun striking them like a blacksmith skidding sparks off the iron on his anvil.

We were heading directly in from the sea toward our island destination. Dramatically, fog was banked along the face of the island and I still couldn't see the glacier that would be pushing out to meet us. The fog was so heavy that it looked like a thick white cloud that had slipped its mooring and fallen to earth, or a billowing four-alarm fire, where only the smoke and the foundation remained.

It curled and eddied along the shoreline, blanking out several miles of vision. I gave a silent prayer of thanks that we hadn't encountered fog like that when we were moving through the ice pack.

Sigurd Dal stood at my elbow talking about Nordaustlandet, saying that because of the difficult ice conditions the island was not accessible at all points every year and could be circumnavigated only when conditions were favorable, which they rarely were. Lying directly northeast of Spitsbergen it was seldom approached by anyone except seal hunters in specially constructed sixty-foot cruisers, and few of them risked it because of the ice caps that rode the island, making the shoreline treacherous.

"The Vestfonna, Austfonna, Sørfonna, and Glitnefonna," Dal said soberly. "Ice up to seven hundred meters high. On the south and east they push into the sea with a big ice wall."

Like the curtain being raised on a stage, as we came closer to the island the fog lifted in segments. The ice stood fifty feet high, I thought. Then, as we came closer, it raised to one hundred feet. With the sun on it, scarves of fog wrapped around it; amazed at its enormity, I wasn't certain of its height, but I knew for sure that it would easily dwarf the Great Wall of China from which this monster edging out to sea got its name.

And this land of silence wasn't silent when you got close to one of the big glaciers. There was a constant crackling, like a giant ice crusher at work, coming from the many-layered structure of the glacier, caused, Dal told me, by the compressed air bubbles, once trapped in the glacier, being released as the ice calved into the sea. I could see some of those dangerous calves being born, one of which had sunk the *Titanic*, and heard the roar as they hit the water with a thunderous splash, the impact like a depth bomb.

I had seen Hereford calves born in a meadow, and without stretching the imagination too much, there was a certain similarity: the big mother, the calf dropping out on the ground. So perhaps the name wasn't so farfetched as I had thought when we came through the pack ice. It did indeed look like the glacier was giving birth to living little glaciers. When the calved ice hit the water it seemed alive, bobbing, going under, then spinning away in a current, the sun picking out a burning blue in the now slow-moving ice.

We anchored off the island and went ashore in the *Jolle*, moving around large, tabular icebergs, bobbing like incredible ice cubes. As we got close to shore the vertical edge of the glacier seemed to tower three hundred feet, blue-green ice reflecting light in electric sparks of rose, violet, magenta. Several muddy streams roared from beneath the glacier.

It was like standing on the edge of creation, watching the world move into life. This is what it had all been once; we had come into existence from under that mountain of ice after it moved ponderously forward shaping the earth in its own brute force design.

We were able to get in to shore and maneuver around, looking for a place where we could climb up on the glacier where the captain wanted to show me the mysterious creatures that lived in the ice.

It wasn't easy. We finally approached that rock of ice from the side, looking for and finding what Dal called sun cups, formed by summer melt, large rough cusps looking like fangs biting through the ice, indentations that enabled us to get up on the glacier, somewhat like climbing a slippery ladder.

The sight from the top was frightening from either view: straight out to sea, where it looked like a lost, endless expanse, or back across that bare ice that stretched as far as the eye could see, fog puffing over it like signal smoke, needing no work by the imagination to know what the Ice Age was all about when glacial giants like this one were astride the land. Glaciers, from two to ten thousand feet thick, had so much weight and grinding power that they dug great lakes, moved entire river systems, wore away mountains, gouged valleys, bulldozed hills into plains.

These mountains of ice held so much water that the sea level in less frigid areas was lowered over two hundred feet, and because of the cold that resulted, snow lines lowered four thousand feet below what they are today.

Without glaciers there would be no Great Lakes in America; our eastern mountains would be much loftier and rockier; New England wouldn't be so stony and infertile; the Middle West's soil wouldn't be so rich; the Ohio, Mississippi, and Missouri rivers would be somewhere else.

What else do you think about when you stand high on a glacier, in a land still dominated by them? For one thing you are surprised that it isn't colder. The sun was high, but wasn't melting the enormous block of ice beneath us at all. Why wasn't I cold standing on this solid ice? Because, Dal told me, I was being warmed twice. From overhead, but the sun was also bouncing heat off that great block of ice. The reflecting effect was called black radiant heat.

Haakon Godtliebsen was fifty feet from where we stood talking about black heat. He called to tell us to come over and see someone else who was enjoying that heat.

At his feet were about a dozen worms, looking much like the common earthworm. Except there was nothing common about these. They could be the most uncommon form of life on earth.

Incredibly, those worms lived permanently in glacier ice. Haakon told me that the worm was so widely celebrated in Norwegian stories and folklore that people who didn't know considered them mythical creatures like the unicorn.

Nudging one into a wiggle with his boot, he said they had the most astounding environment of any creature, spending their entire life cycle close to the freezing point of water. They feed on algae and pollen forced into the snow and ice by wind and concentrated at the surface by melting.

He said that in the fall when the temperature dropped and penetrated the ice the worm went deep into the glacier. Then when spring arrived and warmed the ice the worm rose to the surface, in the summer often coming out of the ice as they had today.

"You can tell a true glacier by these worms," the captain said. "They live only in permanent ice and snow, never in annual snowfields." He looked at me. "Few people have ever seen them."

And few people have ever seen a Svalbard bird rock either, he told me as we went down the glacier, snowy ice-fang by fang. "Even the big ornithologists," he said as we reached the bottom. "Not many want to come this far north. There are bird rocks other places, but nothing like these of Svalbard where the birds are rarely if ever disturbed."

Going back to the *Havella* in the *Jolle* he said that there was a big bird rock up the coast a ways. We'd take a look at that, have a special dinner, and maybe Hansen would even play some music for us.

"Tomorrow," the captain said, "we will get to your lost lake. If we are lucky." He turned to Dal, asking his opinion.

"I think so," Dal said slowly. "Last two summers have been warm. Lots of melt. Look at the sun cups on that glacier we just saw. Sure sign of big melts. I'm betting that the fjord will be open."

For the first time we talked of our destination by name. If we were in luck, farther along these cliffs of ice a glacier had moved into the sea leaving a fjord open, Duvefjorden. We would sail up that to a cove, Duve Bay, "Pigeon Bay," named for a large flock of resident ivory gulls that looked like white pigeons. Beyond that was our lake.

There was open water not far from the shoreline of the island, as Dal had hoped there would be. We moved slowly along that water lane looking for the bird rock that was not far away. Actually, we didn't have to look, only listen.

We heard it from two miles away, like several sirens screaming fire. As we drew closer it was deafening.

Take all the gulls you have seen in a lifetime, multiply that by ten thousand and you'll have a rough idea of a Svalbard bird rock. This large cliff was covered with at least one hundred thousand birds, perhaps more; it was difficult to judge, and also difficult to identify species. They were all gulls, but of many varieties and ages. There were white birds, black and white birds, slate gray gulls, fuzzy yellow young on nests, half-grown birds staggering along ledges, here and there a fight, the flurry of feathers, the slashing of beaks, birds breeding, parents feeding young. That giant rock was living feather.

"It is forbidden to shoot near these bird rocks," the captain said. "We also are not supposed to use the ship's hooter until we are five nautical miles from the rocks."

As we stood watching I saw a large bird come sailing in high. Then the birds on the rock went mad.

"Skua," the captain said grimly. "Giant gull. The biggest. Preys on smaller gulls, especially the young."

The cliff erupted. It looked like it was going to fly across the sea. Birds heaved themselves over the edge, smashing into one another, colliding in midair. Climbing into the sky, they met in a great screaming mass over their bird rock. I have never seen such insane panic among any living creatures.

The skua? He lazily flapped his wings until he was high above the gulls, then he took off down the coast as fast as he could.

"I never saw that before," Haakon Godtliebsen said softly. "Something new whenever we come here."

We watched the birds quiet down and go back to their ledges and nests and then we continued along the coast, leaving the din of the bird rock miles behind.

Two hours later, anchored in quiet ice-free water, we had a

special dinner. The eider ducks Alf Olsen had bagged had been left hanging in feather for several days. Like beef, game—and Aage Rutwold said especially ducks—needed to hang to age and tenderize. Not, he said, the way the British believe, until the bird falls off the string on which it hangs, and is on the edge of decomposition. But hang they must, or they will be tough.

These eiders Aage gently poached in consomme and vegetables until they were just tender, then he lightly rubbed them with honey and put them into the oven until they were brown and the skin crisp. The birds came to the table tasting somewhat like Chinese Peking duck, but these were more moist. Aage had also opened a jar of lingenberries, made a corn pudding from canned corn that tasted like a souffle, browned some small potatoes in the pan with the ducks, and broke open a bottle of velvety Pontet Canet, a chateau Bordeaux that I hadn't known was a passenger. It had been opened hours before so it could breathe its benediction on our dinner.

After dinner Harald Hansen honored us with his music. Without any preamble, he went below and came up with an ordinary carpenter's saw and a violin bow.

With the rest of us circled around him, he sat on a folding chair on deck, his bald head cocked to the side, the saw bent between his knees, his old blue eyes snapping behind his glasses, humming as he made music from the gracefully arched steel blade, drawing the bow gently across it.

The captain and Alf Olsen sang. What they lacked in musical harmony they more than made up for in sheer gusto with swinging, short, colorful Norwegian words.

Alf suggested that he translate some of the folk songs so I could join the song fest.

I wrote down some of the words and translations from that sing-in not far from the North Pole. One, *Bissam, Bissam Ban 'e* (Sleep, Sleep, My Baby) was a favorite of Hansen's. We sang it over and over, the musical saw wailing, "Sleep my baby. The kettle is on the fire full of porridge for you. Father is sifting the corn, mother blows in the pretty horn, sister is spinning gold, and your brother is hunting wild animals in the woods. If it's white, bring it home, if it's gray, let it go, but if it's brown, let it wander in the forest."

Another, *Vassro-Fela* (Watercreek Fiddle Was Wooden), was short, lively, and full of beautiful chords faithfully produced by Hansen on his saw.

"The watercreek fiddle was made of wood, it sank in Losna Lake, but was found again beside a bush and now it sounds night and day. *Suli, luli lei.*"

Suli, luli, lei, what a way to end a day. As I went down to my cabin, that strangely beautiful purple light was flowing from the copper disc of sun balanced on the edge of the sky.

15

That perpetual sun that moved in an arc like a rainbow was well up as we made our way along the coastline, the weather calm, the sea running in smooth waveless swells, fog coiling off the ice all along the island as if the shoreline were afire. Rocky fjords slashed the coast, some were open, some brimming with ice.

I would never get used to the fact that we were sailing an ocean unblemished by other ships. So far up here we had had the Arctic Ocean and even the Barents Sea to ourselves. Tourists didn't know Svalbard existed; there were no smokestack smudges on the horizon, and we hadn't even sighted a plane. Visitors by land, sea, or air were unusual, man was the rarity.

Yet this land lost at the top of the world was one of stirring beauty, its isolation keeping its majesty and serenity secure. True, beauty is in the eye of the beholder, but I doubt that even the pragmatic would be untouched by this silent, sleeping beauty, still unawakened by the twentieth century.

And if this was serene, I wondered again what that

untouched lake and the area around it would be like. It is difficult to project the mind into a singular situation such as that, for not only was it a remarkable one, but it still seemed impossible, even here where birds, seals, polar bears, and foxes were the population. But I had stood on ice that had created the situation and felt its massive power of persuasion.

The crew, surprising me, had talked excitedly about what they would do when we got to the lost lake, not at all blasé as I had thought that they would be. They, too, had never been to a place man hadn't touched for over a decade. They were accustomed to this unspoiled land, but although we hadn't seen them here, others were sometimes on these waters, still some sealers and trappers, occasionally some Russian ships, farther south the coal barges and cod trawlers.

Sigurd Dal began the speculation about the lake. He was a fisherman; it was more than a hobby, it was almost an obsession. He gabbed away like a boy about the fish that might be in the lake.

"Think of it!" he said eagerly. "There could be char there that have never been disturbed."

What were char?

Dal said that they were sometimes called Spitsbergen salmon, but that they were really Arctic Ocean fish, *Salvelinus alpinus,* which themselves differ from *Salmo,* salmon and trout. But, like salmon, the regular sea-run char also leave the ocean and swim up rivers and fjords to breed. Sometimes these ocean char then enter lakes and establish freshwater colonies. In Svalbard, Dal said, as if talking about hidden gold mines, there are isolated colonies in lakes that the fish had entered during glacial times. These secluded lake char have become a distinct species, similar to trout but more vividly colored.

"They are like no other fish, these char in glacial lakes," Dal said reverently. "Their backs are olive and they have beautiful ts on their sides, ranging from rust, red, and pink to bright nge. Bellies run from pink to scarlet, so some call them red ir. In breeding males all colors are vivid as fresh paint. You ›uldn't believe that these fish were once like the char here in ꞉ ocean that are dull silver with little spots you can hardly see."

So Dal was hoping these spectacular char would be in the ꞉e, and he thought aloud about what Aage would do with those h in his galley. Haakon Godtliebsen was going to fill some ,ottles with the lake's pure water. Alf Olsen proved his age by stating that he would chisel his name in stone for posterity; Harald Hansen would try to bring wild flowers in their unpolluted soil to transplant in his windowboxes in Tromsø, hoping that the wild, unspoiled strain would take. I thought of the rare experience of drinking in air that hadn't been used. Aage had no comment, except to echo Dal's hope that these very special char would be in that lake. What would he do with them if they were? His eyes twinkled. "Fish like those cook themselves," he said. "I've never had one, but I've heard about them." That was a long conversation for Aage Rutwold, so obviously he too was caught up in the excitement of this visit to a never-never land where no man had been for so long.

Alf was at the wheel, the captain at the deck rail with binoculars slowly glassing the coastline. Dal, as usual, was at the bow, but he was coasting, as there was little ice in our path. Aage and Hansen were at the rail beside me.

My feeling as we approached the focal point of this journey was not easy to describe. It was a mixture. I have said that my discovery that the seeking is more rewarding than the finding has rubbed off some of life's rough spots. So it was on this trip, the seeking had made the focal point fade, until now when it was sharply in focus again I wondered what the finding would bring that I hadn't already experienced.

We all stood silently now as the captain watched for signs of the fjord that had been iced in.

Finally, glasses still at his eyes, when he quietly said, "We have luck. Duvefjorden is open," I actually felt my heart miss a beat or two and sweat spring out on the palms of my hands.

There was some ice on the steep rock sides of the fjord we entered, sending long arms down its sides, glistening in the sun like molten steel. We went along that calm water that had stolen in from the sea, up the narrow rocky chasm. The white birds were there as we came from the long tongue of the fjord into Duve Bay, mist rising in gunsmoke puffs, the high reaches beyond a glistening palace of ice. Swooping close over our heads, dozens of small ivory gulls shrilled "Keer! Keer!" as we anchored in the middle of the little bay.

There was almost a fistfight when Dal discovered that Hansen had forgotten to bring fishing rods. There was plenty of line and spinning lures, but no rods. Alf Olsen finally solved the problem with empty aquavit bottles, winding line around the body of the bottle, using the neck to throw the line out. He demonstrated to a grumpy Dal. Hansen went below and found a big cane pole he would use.

This fussing around was upsetting me. My mouth was dry. The keening birds made me nervous. It seemed to me that it took the captain a long time to react. He had brought us here; it was his move. I felt like jumping overboard and swimming ashore.

Finally the crew got the *Jolle* ready to lower over the side. The captain touched my shoulder and pointed toward shore. A streak flashed there, a rush of white light, a tiny stream coming from fresh water inland, our lost glacial lake without a name.

As we started for shore in the *Jolle*, Alf Olsen rowing, awfully slowly, it seemed to me, I tried to shake off the feeling that we were about to poach this precious silence, vandalize it.

As Alf rowed, I remembered a long-ago English class, conducted by a professor who liked to spark discussion with an arbitrary remark that catapulted us into conversation, sometimes a tangled one, knotted by disagreement and too many of us trying to talk at once. The professor usually brought us back to his original remark, clarifying the situation.

Once he wasn't successful. At least I thought he wasn't. I was the reason. I completely disagreed with him.

He began the discussion by reading from a modern novel, *The Caine Mutiny*, I believe, quoting, " 'It was a moment of pure silence.' " Putting the book down he said, "This is a writer who doesn't use language properly." He then picked up Webster's Dictionary and read, " 'Silence. The condition or quality of being or keeping silent; avoidance of speech or noise. The absence of sound; stillness.' "

Looking keenly at us (I remember still that he had the bright, staring eyes of a goshawk), he said, "I maintain that silence is neither pure nor impure. It is simply the absence of sound. Discussion, please. Raise hands."

One girl wondered about the hushed, almost sacred cathedral silence; another discussed the morbid silence of the tomb; one spoke of the deathlike silence before dawn.

"Accentuation," the professor said. "It goes back to the original definition—silence is simply the absence of sound."

I raised my hand, disagreeing, going into what I believed then and still do. Gulls crying over a beach, the waves breaking on shore, but no other sound, that is silence, the natural silence of the seashore. In the forest, leaves dropping to the ground, a small creature, perhaps a shrew, scuttling through the underbrush, a woodpecker tapping on a tree, far off the call of a crow, this also is normal silence for that place. Silence makes its own sounds, I said. A river going over rocks, a bat flying in a cave, a duck's wings whistling through dawn light, the wind in the trees on a mountaintop, the rain on the surface of a lake.

The professor stared at me. "Interesting," he said slowly, "but what you are talking about is poetry, not silence."

The class laughed and we turned to another subject.

And now coming up was a silence I had never dreamed was possible. Men are the breakers of silence, and there had been none here for twelve years.

We beached the *Jolle* and walked upstream, heading toward the source of that little stream that ran into the bay. Far left, slopes of snow were streaked, tinted red by moisture running over carboniferous sandstone that jutted out of high ground. Small streams ran under our feet, joining the larger one we were following. The land ahead, ground moraine from the receded glacier, looked like the rubble from a hydrogen bomb attack. The glacier, the top stratum of the ice cap, had advanced with enormous force, upending rocks, ripping the earth. It was like walking across the rocky, pitted bottom of a dead sea.

The isolation was total. The vast barrier of the Arctic Ocean behind us, the towering massif of black, snow-capped mountain before us, rearing across the skies to the north like an immense fortress, the pure, clear air moving around us, the stillness, as if the earth had stopped moving, made this place more a part of heaven than of earth.

Beyond that mountain lay the largely unexplored *Fonna*, land of eternal snow, where it had compacted perhaps two miles thick near the center of the ice mass.

The streams spurting out before us widened now as we quickly moved forward; snow on the ridges and slopes was heavier, and suddenly we were wading in icy water up to our hips. We went up a steep slope that was spilling water like a dam.

Below was the lake. It was the color of the captain's eyes, the blue of sun-struck glacial ice. The sensation was like stepping into a deep but bright cave of instant solitude. The quiet came from the small lake like a physical presence.

A hundred yards from us a pair of brown-beige Arctic foxes, the shyest of the north's animals, stood, ears flicking, walking casually away as we advanced. A flock of eider ducks, among the wariest of all creatures, didn't fluff a reddish-brown feather as we went to the lake shore. They remained placid in a raft in the center of the lake.

Cupped in rock, the water, clear as light through a window, revealed dozens of foot-long green-backed fish, so undisturbed by us that they lay as if frozen in ice. Sigurd Dal's char were here.

All objects were sharply isolated, with the result that there was no confusion in the eye of what was before you. It was like being a small boy again, standing beside a woodland pool identifying objects that floated, starkly exposed in the clearness of the water.

I had the feeling of losing all sense of proportion, of thinking that something vital to mankind was being born in this cocoon of isolation. Silence wove a net around me, and as I stood caught by it, not wanting to even scuff a foot to break out of it, I thought that I finally understood what Leonardo da Vinci had meant when he said, "If you are alone, you are your own man."

I had a sudden clearness of mind, a mind that was dropping its problems like invisible litter. Could mind-cleansing despoil this place?

The captain, still leading us, stopped his hitching stride, and held up a hand, pointing. We saw movement ahead, a gray shape advancing across the rock-strewn landscape. A young reindeer, antlers in velvet.

We stood still, and the animal, never having seen a human, came within thirty feet, sniffing, cocking its head. It stepped calmly aside as we went on.

Hansen, the gardener, pointed out the phenomenon of flowers sprouting from rocks, saxifrage, petals like drops of blood, delicate yellow dwarf Arctic poppies, lacey red licebane, mountain avens running in burning white lines.

Hansen motioned to me and I went over to where he was hunkered beside Arctic poppies that seemed to be pushing out of sheer rock. He explained how these wildflowers could grow with almost no soil under them. Poking a finger under a poppy he pointed out its "cushion" made from leaves of previous years. Rate of decay in polar ground is slow, so there could be ten years of leaves in each flower cushion. They were brown, damp, still attached to the crown of the taproot, the moisture they collected was held where the plant needed it. Other moisture came from light snowfalls, ice and frost in the top few inches of the ground which was melted by summer sun. Hansen marveled aloud at the fact that these hardy flowers pack three seasons into one, completing their cycles in about six weeks, survive through the long dark winter when temperatures drop way below zero.

"They are," he said quietly, "the hardiest seed-bearing plants in existence."

He walked me over to a shelf of rust-colored rock back from the lake and peeled some lichen from it. The lichen colors the rocks, he told me, its acid enabling it to stubbornly cling to the smooth surface. Lichen didn't need soil, Hansen said, but it did help cultivate soil so plants could grow.

Hansen left me then, ambling off away from the lake, his head down searching for flowers.

I hurried to catch up with the captain, who was walking along the lake shore. He stopped, watching the fish slowly fin through the clear water. Suddenly, as if Haakon standing beside me had struck me with an ax, I had a headache that split straight through my skull. I touched my head, wincing.

Haakon noticed. "Headache?"

At my nod, he said, "You are a polluted man. I am surprised you haven't had one before this. This happens sometimes in the far north. The air is so pure, that until you get used to it, it is like taking too much aquavit too fast. There has been no one breathing here, using up the air, no disease, no smog, no industry, no automobiles, so you probably are taking in really fresh air for the first time since you were born."

The piercing headache didn't go right away; it was, I suppose, like a deep-sea diver decompressing in stages before he resurfaces. I, the polluted man, was adjusting my breathing in this sea of clean air where I was out of my element.

Without speaking, we fished then, Olsen's aquavit bottles working like small spinning rods, peeling the line off without a problem. We stopped when we caught twelve, just enough for dinner. A bond was understood, as if by some kind of osmosis, that we would not take advantage of this lake.

The char were as Dal had described them, slimmer than salmon, larger than brook trout, spotted with red and gold; three were orange, dotted with deep red. Aage reverently placed them on a ledge of snow until we were ready to leave.

As if in a cathedral, we kept our silence, each man did what he had in his mind; Alf went to find a high rock on which to chisel his name; Aage and Sigurd Dal stood watching the fish flashing like jewels in the hard, clear water. Haakon limped to the other side of the lake to fill two gallon bottles. Would he believe, as the Hindus believed of the Ganges, that this pure water would stay forever fresh in the bottles? Would he also use it to sprinkle on the newborn, the newly married, the sick? Did he believe that a single drop of this water, perhaps made holy by being untouched by man, when dropped on the eyelids of the dying would immediately purify them?

Hansen was still off inspecting the flowers that he hoped to transplant; and I, the headache going, sat high on a rock overlooking the lake, in communion with myself for the first time. The amazing aspect of this place wasn't in anything physical. It was in the first pure silence that I have ever known.

We seemed to be separated from the world by a wall of air that washed around us as sweet as spring water. Not one of us spoke. We were mesmerized by the tranquillity. I had a sudden longing to stay here until I could come to terms with myself, and try to understand what nature can do when not tampered with. It could bring peace, I was certain. Even to a man polluted by more than soiled air and water.

The sudden shout shattered the silence and the thought, making me realize the impossibility of both. It was Hansen calling from the direction of the bay.

We converged, walking rapidly toward the sound of his voice. Hansen was standing in the center of a circle of rocks. He bent and picked up a tarnished brass button, the sun making it wink like a diamond.

Surrounding Hansen were buttons, heels of boots, rotting bills of caps. We all bent, examining pieces of gray uniforms, the rusted remains of a short-wave radio.

Haakon Godtliebsen finally straightened. "Nazis," he said, not speculating upon how they died, whether they had been trapped behind a glacier, or where their remains were. He just said, in a voice I didn't recognize with its quiet venom, that these arctic waters had enabled the Nazis to make their main U-boat thrusts, also helped them open up a wider coastline to counter the enemy blockade. This northern lane also gave them access to Sweden's iron ore that had helped make the Nazi war possible. The world of worry, war, and men was with us again. How did the soldiers get here? How long had they stayed? Had they died? How?

We all heard the faint sound at the same time. Something, or someone, was watching us. We turned as one.

Less than twenty-five yards from us were six reindeer, noses twitching curiously. The Arctic fox and his vixen were also there, bright eyes on us. There were no enemies here. This was the peaceable kingdom, where man had not yet had the opportunity to create fear.

When we moved, the animals calmly turned and walked across the moonscape of the scraped and rutted glacial moraine, fading away over the nearest rise like figures in a dream. At the top of the stony mound one reindeer stopped, swiveled its head, stared at us for several seconds, then vanished.

No one spoke. Stopping at the edge of the lake, we stood watching the char in the crystal clear water, moving with slow, stately, almost ballet movements, not the fin-twitching, nervous darting of all of the other game fish that I had observed. The sun speared deep in the water, making the spots on the char flash like amethysts and rubies.

That sun was high, glinting on the forbidding frozen-in land rising cloudlike beyond, and suddenly I was struck with the reality of the situation, of exactly where I was. Before, it had seemed that my mind had stood apart from all of this, taking it in but not summing it up.

It was disturbingly clear, to have true silence, peace, no fear, genuine tranquillity, you had to completely leave the world of men. I had come thousands of miles to do exactly that. And for several hours, despite the fact that there were five men with me, there had been a quietness deep inside me that I had never known before, and probably would never know again. It was like trudging mile after mile through the deep gloom of a pine forest and then suddenly breaking out of the trees into the sunlight. Like swimming underwater until you thought your lungs would burst, then surfacing and filling your whole being with that sweet, life-giving oxygen.

The reward wasn't just in finding this lake, unseen by men

for all of those years, but in the journey itself, getting to know these quiet, confident men of the *Havella*, untouched by a world spinning in confusion. In an age where utter dependence upon civilization and all of its complications was enslaving most of us, their values were based on the solid bedrock of free spirit. To know that there still are such men and a place like this land at the top of the world was in itself salvation and deliverance of a kind.

We spent the day at the lake. But Hansen had unwittingly broken its spell. We sat silently over the lunch Aage had brought, each man's mind racing with private thoughts. Few in Norway had been unmarked by the Nazi war, and Hansen's discovery here where it was least expected touched raw spots. Even on me. I had been deeply involved in that war.

As if to tell us that we were unwanted here, a pair of Arctic terns kept dive-bombing us, coming mere inches from our heads, then veering away, screeching. We moved, but the birds kept chattering at us, noisy as wrens. I wondered why we hadn't disturbed them before. Why had it taken them that long to discover that our strangeness spelled danger? Were they also mesmerized by the tranquillity?

Finally Aage went to the ledge of snow and collected the char that we had caught and we walked across the rough stone rubble and through the cold streams rushing into the little bay and took the *Jolle* back to the *Havella*.

Standing on deck, watching the high land around the lake vanish, the sun shedding its strange purple light over it, I suddenly realized that I had gained something immensely valuable. I had acquired a memory more precious than money in the bank. When life became difficult it was a memory that I could reach into and spend again and again. A memory of a journey into silence that would give me many future moments of peace.

As the *Havella* sailed out of the fjord linking the bay with that lost land beyond, the Ivory gulls' *keer keer* cries followed us until we reached the sea. It was a sound that I would hear on the threshold of many a dream.

INDEX

Amundsen, Roald, 3, 6, 23–26, 27, 41, 51, 86, 93, 94–98, 172
Andrée, Salomon August, 123
Andrews, Roy Chapman, 115–116
Archer, Colin, 31
Arntzen, Kristian, 67–68

Baldwin, Fred, 89–91, 92
Barents, Willem, 7
Bennett, Steven, 80
birds, 43–44, 103–109, 137–140, 142, 182–183, 197, 198
black radiant heat, 181
Bolin, Wilhelm, 17–19, 20, 23, 41, 50, 67, 69, 93, 100
Byrd, Richard E., 6, 95, 98

char, lake, 187–188, 192, 194, 196, 197

Chinese Wall Front Glacier, 1, 2, 56
cod, 84–85

De Long, George W., 26–27
Devonshire, 15
Døgnavild, 19
Douglas, William O., 10

Ellsworth, Lincoln, 25, 94–95, 96

flowers, 193
foxes, Arctic, 156–158, 192, 196
Fram expedition, 30–38
Franklin, John, 23

glaciers, 51–52, 53–56, 178–181
Gordon, James H., 117, 118–119
Gresswell, R. Kay, 52–56
Guilibaud, Rene, 97
Gulf Stream, 81, 82, 161–166

Hartviksen, Karl, 20
headaches, "pollution," 193–194
Herz, George, 1–3, 4–6, 7–8, 9, 43
Hillary, Edmund, 50–51

Ibsen, Henrik, 101
ice, types of, 103, 168, 169–176

Jackson, Frederick, 38
Johansen, Hjalmar, 33–38

lake (destination), description of, 191–192
Landnámabok, 6–7
Lapps, 11–12
Longyear, John, 62
Lyngen, 16, 18, 40–71 *passim*, 161, 164

McClintock, Leopold, 28
MacMillan, Donald, 114
Menzel, Donald H., 119–120
Mills, Enos A., 115
mirages, 113–121
Mohn, Henrik, 27
Monge, Gaspard, 117
mørketiden (murky time), 19–20
musk ox, 73–79

Nansen, Fridtjof, 3, 6, 26, 27–39, 41, 51, 93, 98, 172

Nazis, at lake, 195, 197
Nelson, E. W., 78
Nobile, Umberto, 25–26, 94–97, 98
Norwegian food, 48–50, 112, 184

Peary, Robert E., 3, 6, 25, 30, 95, 114, 119, 133
polar bears, 89, 90, 91, 134–136, 140–150, 154
Pytheas of Massilia, 6

regelation, 54–55
reindeer, 192, 196
Rudi, Henry, 22

Scoresby, William, Jr., 116
Scott, Falcon, 116, 130
seals, 80–81, 87, 89, 125–132
seasickness, 163–164
Stefansson, Vilhjalmur, 143
Svedrup, Otto, 31, 33, 38

Tirpitz, 15

Viking explorations, 69–71

Wellman, Walter, 7
Whittaker, James, 4
Wood, R. W., 118
worms, glacier-dwelling, 181–182